Your Garden in the West C

Compiled by: Jane Costin
John Wilson
Mervyn Woodward

Edited by: James Lawrence

CONTENTS

Back cover photograph by Cliff Webb of Clemens Photography, Bodmin.

Published by
Bracken Publishing
Bracken House, 199A Holt Road
Cromer, Norfolk NR27 9JN

ISBN 1 871614 17 1

Printed by Broadgate Printers, Aylsham, Norfolk

November 1993

Introduction

On a recent visit to Sweden I asked my Swedish host what came to mind when he heard speak of England. He answered without hesitation: "Football, pubs and country gardens." I think he was being a little generous about the first (unless he was referring to our hooligans), but there can be no doubt we are "world champions" of the other two. Nothing better defines Englishness, at least its kinder face, than the country pub and the country garden; they somehow seem part and parcel of the same benign character.

Our series of regional pub guides, covering the south of England, is already well established, and so it seemed only natural to complement this with a similar series devoted to the garden. Friends and associates were sceptical: "But there are already thousands of books about gardening!" they protested. True, but that just shows how obsessed the English are with the subject. If further evidence were needed, look at the way garden centres have mushroomed over the past 20 years. Visiting them has become a leisure activity in itself.

And from there the concept grew: not only was this to be a guide to gardens to visit, but also to garden centres. Furthermore, growing conditions vary from region to region, so there is a need for a guide, written by local experts, about how to make a success of your garden in the West Country. Most of what you buy for your garden comes from local suppliers, and many of the best of these are featured. In short, it is not only (I hope) an attractive guide book but handy for reference also. As far as I am aware, this has not been done before.

But why are the English such a nation of gardeners? It surely springs from our rural roots, still there despite 200 years of industrialisation. In truth, we don't really like our big cities very much, but yearn instead for the proverbial rose-strewn thatched cottage set in a Constable landscape. If we can't have that we can at least pretend a little; hence the neatly tended little patches of countryside which are the hallmark of suburbia.

We also have the ideal climate to fuel our escapism. We may grumble, but it is a kindly one as far as plants are concerned, and there are few others in which it is possible to grow alpines and Scandinavian pines alongside Mediterranean or even sub-tropical species. And no other region matches the West Country in this regard: the mild, frost-free winters of the far south west allow so much more exotic diversity than the less blessed parts to the north and east. Although the winters are more bracing 'up-country', the soils and general growing conditions make it one of England's prime horticultural areas.

The very word 'garden' derives from the Persian for 'paradise.' I hope this book will assist you in the enjoyment of our many little corners of paradise, here in this fortunate part of the world.

I would also like to hear from you if you should come across any lovely garden, interesting garden centre, or a supplier who has given good service. All letters will be gratefully acknowledged, and those which I find especially helpful will be awarded a complimentary copy of the second edition.

JAMES LAWRENCE

Foreword

The peninsular of the South West of England is of course bordered on two of its three sides by water, and no spot is more than 25 miles from the coast (although one may be a little further "up country" in Wiltshire and parts of Somerset and Dorset). Thus there are areas exposed to gales and salt-laden winds, but when protected a very wide range of plants can be grown in the maritime climate. The region is home to numerous fine gardens, large and small, many of which are internationally renowned for their beauty and wealth of plants. Whilst a large part of the South West is centred around granite, there are many areas of sand, clay, peat loam and river or estuarine soils, increasing the range of plants which may be grown.

The region has a very high proportion of retired and elderly people, and above average numbers of enthusiastic gardeners. There are more glasshouses, conservatories and patios per head of population than in any other area of the United Kingdom. Where better to indulge in the garden delights of tending your own plot or visiting other gardens, nurseries, horticultural suppliers or garden centres. This book promises to help guide you further into the wondrous world of gardening, and help you achieve greater success and enjoyment in your gardening endeavours.

Terry Underhill

3

From the Same Publisher

May be obtained at most good bookshops and some pubs within the region, or by writing to Bracken Publishing.

£3.50

£3.50

£3.50

£3.50

£4.00

Prices include postage etc. No orders accepted without prior payment, other than from recognised retailers.

Conservatories

Conservatories

"A conservatory is to be considered an absolute necessity in connection with the home of taste", says Shirley Hibberd in his book 'Rustic Adornments for Homes of Taste'. 'Connection' is to be taken literally, for he frowned upon the idea of a conservatory being anything other than part of the house, physically connected to it.

The Victorian age was the heyday of the conservatory, when it was seen as a place of romance, a rendezvous and an escape. But its origins can be traced to late 16th century England, when citrus fruits were first introduced. However, they were little more than heated sheds to shelter the tender plants through the winter. Glass was used from the early 17th century in orangeries, though roofs were still solid, but gradually it became understood that plants required more light, so the glass roof came into vogue. One of the earliest of these constructions, built in 1704, still stands at Kensington Palace.

Originally built from masonry and wood, with the development of glass and cast iron conservatories sometimes evolved into magnificent palaces, such as those at Chatsworth and Alton Towers. In time, the fashion spread to humbler homes, and indeed throughout the world, although Britain remained the recognised leader in the field.

The Victorians turned the conservatory into a place of entertainment and relaxation, much as we understand it today. It affords we stuffy Northern Europeans a chance to briefly escape our grey, temperate climate and bask, for a while, in the tropics, heady with the fragrance and lushness of exotic plants.

Where do I start?

A conservatory is much more than a glass box stuck on the side of a house. It will be a fairly expensive item, so much consideration should go into your choice of size, style and materials, furnishing, flooring and plants. Perhaps most important is to make sure you are dealing with reputable suppliers, such as are featured in these pages. Going for the cheapest quote does not always mean you are getting the best deal. (Quality suppliers often complain, with justification, that they take a lot of trouble and expense drawing up plans for a customer, even securing planning permission, only to lose the business to a less scrupulous merchant who undercuts the price and uses those same plans for his own benefit. If there are unethical traders about, there are also many unethical customers.)

A true professional will be happy to advise you on the size and style of your conservatory, and draw up plans accordingly. As for materials, there are basically three types available.

Materials

1 uPVC

Most smaller conservatories are constructed from this material. In larger sizes it should be supported by steel.

The main disadvantage of uPVC is that it is susceptible to movement. Remember, in winter the temperature outside may be close to zero, but inside it could be as high as 30°C. The result is considerable outward pressure – the roof must be reinforced. Snow loading is another factor, and down draughts can also exert significant force.

On the other hand, uPVC is very versatile and virtually maintenance-free.

2 Aluminium

Most commercial conservatories are constructed from this material. It is strong and rigid (look for quality thin aluminium as in greenhouses), though not of itself attractive. Box-sectioned aluminium looks better, and polyester powder coating can be any colour.

It is advisable to have the aluminium thermally broken – that is separating the outside metal from the inside to combat condensation.

3 *Timber*

Most larger domestic conservatories are constructed from this material. A living material, wood is perhaps aesthetically the most pleasing, but is also very versatile and strong. If properly treated it is very stable and requires minimal maintenance.

A popular hardwood is Brazilian mahogany. If concerned about the Amazon rain forest you could choose a loosely based mahogany from the Far East, or perhaps a temperate hardwood such as oak, but most 'eco-friendly' are the laminated softwoods from unendangered, managed northern forests. These are also extremely robust and cheaper.

Heating and Ventilation

It is a common mistake, usually in an effort to keep down costs, to neglect proper ventilation or protection from the sun. The result, particularly in south-facing conservatories, is an oven. Temperatures can soar to danger levels, which neither plant nor animal life can survive. Your conservatory has become unusable for much of the summer, and so is almost a complete waste of money.

Rooflights are, therefore, highly desirable, and an extractor fan is to be recommended in conservatories with a southerly aspect. Roof blinds are a must, and should be of a solar-reflective material.

One must also consider how the conservatory is to be heated in winter if one is not to lose all those precious plants. Perhaps the

Photo courtesy Marston & Langinger Ltd.

greatest boon of a conservatory is to be able to enjoy those sunny days when it is too cold to sit out, but pleasantly warm under glass (even without extra heating). It induces a wonderful feeling of well-being in the depths of a miserable winter.

Blinds

These will protect not only you and your plants from fierce sunlight, but also your flooring, furniture and fitments. At the same time as 'softening' the atmosphere they also afford greater privacy. Blinds are most effective fitted to the entire roof area, leaving ventilators clear. They need not be purely functional, but can also be decorous, a finishing touch to your conservatory.

The traditional blind is made of Pinoleum, a durable material (manufactured mostly in France) consisting of pine reeds sewn together with high quality treated cotton, the edges finely bound. These are attractive and provide approx. 70% shading.

Holland blinds are made of stiffened cotton treated with a preservative. They are of lighter appearance, especially suitable for conservatories used as extra rooms in the house, where there may be fewer plants.

Heating

One can use electric or oil heaters as in a greenhouse (q.v.), but the advantage of a conservatory is that, being attached to the house, it is easy to extend the central heating, in the form of radiators or underfloor pipes. This is the commonest method.

Arguably the most effective and elegant solution is to build in heating grilles in the floor. These may be cast iron, and can be made to blend in with flooring tiles. They are laid over a channel housing finned pipes connected to the central heating. Apart from taking up no space at all, they have two great advantages: 1) water may be 'damped down' through the grilles, giving off steam – plants will love it; 2) they can be operated in conjunction with electric ventilators, providing a constant, regulated environment regardless of what is going on outside.

Photo courtesy Marston & Langinger Ltd.

Furniture and Flooring

Two kinds of furniture are most commonly seen in conservatories:–

1 *Cane*. Simple and elegant, these come mostly from Malaysia. They are sturdy, lightweight and durable, but require thick cushioning to sit on. For this reason they are not suitable for use outdoors. Some are designed to swivel. Available in light or dark cane.

2 *Wicker*. This is the one for traditionalists. They are still made from willow by craftsmen in Norfolk. Lighter even than cane, wicker is also very strong and is weather-resistant, so that it may be left outside. They can be quite comfortable even without cushions. The only maintenance required is the occasional brushing or a wash with warm soapy water. Available in several finishes and colours.

When planning, you should consider how your furniture will blend with the flooring, and the conservatory itself, to create the overall impression which you are seeking.

Flooring tiles come in an enormous range of colours, textures and shapes, but can be summarised as follows:–

1 *Terracotta*. Inexpensive, available old or new, rustic or fine, huge range of shapes, sizes and colours.

2 *Slate*. Wonderful natural texture, beautiful colour combinations of blue-purple, grey, russet, buff and rust.

3 *Sandstone*. Traditional Yorkstone flags or more sophisticated finely finished squares.

4 *Mosaics*. Handmade from tiles or glass, either as border or central feature.

5 *Tessellated and encaustic tiles*. Bold colours and patterns as favoured by Victorians.

Pictures courtesy
Marston & Langinger Ltd.

Tessellated and encaustic tiles

Planting Ideas

Everything is now ready for the final stage: choosing the plants for your conservatory – it is just not complete without them. The opportunities are endless; although many conventional houseplants will thrive under glass, you can grow exotic plants that are too big for the house, or require alot of light, or that can't cope with too much central heating. Plants too tender for a normal greenhouse will readily grow in a conservatory, though one is advised not to get too ambitious; a hot-house plant struggling to make it through the winter will not be an attractive feature.

For a new conservatory, fast-growers (especially climbers) are a good idea. Morning glory, black-eyed Susan, Cobea scandens and ivy are all safe bets. Bulbs are also very easy to grow, and often provide scent, but may need to be removed from the conservatory during their dormant periods.

If facing south, plants like bougainvillea, plumbago or orleander should do well; if north, try aspidistras, chlorophytums, ferns and foliage plants. Remember to select plants that will give you all-year-round greenery – jasmine, for example, which also brings forth the most lusciously scented blooms in spring.

Plants which require dampness (eg Grass of the Nile, Papyrus) are an asset. It is impossible to over-water them, and the humidity is of benefit to other plants.

Finally, don't overlook hanging baskets – they add a further dimension, and offer scope for some lovely trailing plants. Geraniums and petunias are old favourites, but you could try convulvulus arvensis or ivy-leaved pelargoniums. A good garden centre will offer interesting alternatives.

Picture courtesy Marston & Langinger Ltd.

Convolvulus Arvensis

Greenhouses

Greenhouses

Growing under glass opens up a whole new dimension in the garden. In creating an artificial Mediterranean or even tropical environment, one can grow quite exotic flowers or fruits, bring forward native plants, or greatly increase the prospects of successful propagation.

Small frames can fulfill some of these purposes, but the limited volume of air makes temperature control quite difficult. Lack of headroom precludes taller plants, and of course they are more difficult for the gardener to work in.

Greenhouses are of three main types: lean to, span-roof and circular. The latter are attractive and compact, and may be regarded as part of garden decor, but their small size limits their use, as is the case with frames. Span-roof is the most common type, being completely versatile in terms of size and position. The lean-to greenhouse, which ofcourse needs to be placed against an existing wall, often becomes a virtual conservatory, an extension to the living space of the home, and a very pleasant place to sit on a cold but sunny day in winter.

Heating

A greenhouse should always be placed in a sunny position, but ofcourse in the colder months additional heating will be required to protect tender plants or seedlings (most of which germinate at between 13 - 20°C, or 55 – 68°F).

The simplest and most economical method is to use a propagator inside the greenhouse, thereby creating a little frame with, in effect, its own heating system. However, the young plants will soon outgrow this and so ambient heating is necessary to avoid the shock of a sudden fall in temperature.

Reckon that the cost of heating a greenhouse doubles with every 3°C. For this reason, most are held at a temperature of 7°C (43°F), enough to keep most plants alive, if not always happy! The most common methods used are:–

1 *Electric fan heaters* – convenient and clean, can be used in summer as air circulator, but expensive to run.

2 *Gas burners* – effective, but some harmful gases emitted, so there must be ventilation.

3 *Oil heaters* – must be kept clean, and can become lethal if burning improperly.

4 *Hot water pipes* – the best solution if it's possible, but must be left on at night.

Common Problems Growing Under Glass

Symptoms	Cause	Remedy
poor growth, distorted leaves, yellow blotches	viruses	remove infected plants use insecticides
poor growth, wilting	aphids	malathion, nicotine, primicarb
poor growth, wilting esp. tomatoes & cucumbers	root diseases	change soil
rotting, grey fluffy down	grey mould	better ventilation, benomyl or thiophanate-methyl alternating with captan
leaves bronzing, cobwebs	red spider	keep plants moist use derris or diazinon
tunnels in leaves	leaf miners	remove affected leaves use diazinon, nicotine, HCH
seedlings collapse at base	damping-off	better ventilation, sew thinly in sterile compost, use Cheshunt mixture
wilting leaves and stems	lack of water	watering can!

Enjoying Bonsai

Chinese Elm (50 years old)

Although originating in China, the recognised home of Bonsai is Japan where, over the centuries, the art has been perfected and passed on around the world. For many years the only trees available were outdoor, but recently more and more tropical species, suitable for indoors (where they make a marvellous feature), have appeared.

The cheapest and perhaps most frustrating method (success rate only 5%!) is to grow from seed. This is a long term commitment, and seedlings tend to die when only a year or two old. Most common cause of this is Damping Off Disease, which may be prevented by spraying with Benomyl alternated with a liquid copper fungicide every two weeks. Some seeds need stratifying to begin germination, so that after planting they should be placed in a refrigerator for a while - follow the instructions on the packet.

Much quicker is to take cuttings. The best time for this is late spring, taking from the most vigorous greenwood. Or it may be possible to lift the whole sapling - late autumn or early spring is best. Plant with an open compost in a large pot, and protect from inclement weather until the tree has recovered and is forming new growth.

Some garden centres supply juvenile trees - look for healthy stock, not pot bound, and with a pleasing shape. Mature trees are naturally much more expensive, so choose a dealer who knows what he's talking about and is prepared to spend time with you.

Growing tips

1 If tree becomes pot-bound, repot in the spring, just before buds burst. Conifers may be repotted in autumn. Trim about a third off the root mass to promote growth of hair-like feeder roots.

2 Protect outdoor trees from wind and frost, indoor trees from direct sun.

3 Feed outdoor trees every two weeks from spring to mid-summer, then monthly until autumn. Indoor trees should be fed fortnightly through spring and summer, monthly during autumn and winter. Never feed within one month after potting, or if the tree is in flower or sick.

4 The tree must never be allowed to dry out. Use rainwater or boiled water on indoor trees, although tap water which has been left to acquire room temperature will do. Water by immersing the pot until the surface of the compost is covered, stand until bubbles stop or for approx. 10 mins.

5 Keep misted and well drained. Tree may be stood on pebbles kept moist.

6 It is natural for some trees to lose leaves at certain times, but check that you are carrying out the above, and under leaves for insect attack.

Indoor Plants

by Sue Hodges of Park Garden Centre, Almondsbury, near Bristol.

How does one define indoor plants? They are plants grown indoors either for their ornamental foliage or flowers. They must be able not only to survive but also to grow in the conditions in which we live and work, bearing in mind that these conditions change daily and are not designed for the benefits of the plants. What do plants need to survive and grow? They basically require a high intensity of daylight. Most plants, however, resent direct sunlight in the middle of a summer's day, as this can burn their leaves.

The more green they are the more likely are they to succeed indoors away from light. Variegated and brightly colour species need to be in as light as position as possible. They like circulation of air without being in a draught, so do not leave plants shut in a room. Plants do not like too much fluctuation in temperature, although this is inevitable when central heating is turned off at night. Some plants tolerate central heating better than others, but humidity is something they all miss more than anything. Humidifiers on radiators do help. Where, possible, stand pots on wet pebbles or pack the pots with wet peat and moss in an outer container.

Watering

It is important to know your particular plant's water requirements and to water as often as necessary. Most survive dry periods but more indoor plants die from OVERwatering than from any other cause. A good tip is to take plants to the sink, fill the top of the pot with water, leave to drain, place back on window sill or table, then lift the pot after a few days to get used to the weight of the pot. If heavy, do not water; if light, water, and so on in succession.

Re-potting

You must first see if the plant is pot-bound; that is, whether the soil is a mass of roots with hardly any soil showing. It may also look top heavy for its pot. It may not produce new growth in spring or you may see roots poking through holes in the pot. Re-pot mostly in spring for green plants and as directed for others, using a good houseplant compost.

Feeding

It then becomes necessary to feed the plants when they are growing and producing flowers. The easiest method of giving them food is in the water. There are several proprietary foods on the market.

Pests and Diseases

If you have maintained your plant well it is particularly disturbing when pests and diseases occur. They appear for a variety of reasons not always readily understandable. The most common is that they travel from one plant to another, even from the garden. In other cases they are latent on the plant and the hot, dry atmosphere in the house, or the way that the plant has been looked after, brings them out. Instigate a policy of preventative disinfecting by spraying with insecticide and/or fungicide diluted in water every 14 to 21 days.

Cyclamen

The Pond in Your Garden

There is fascination in water (especially to children!): we are all drawn to it by its movement, sound and life. A stream or pond is a most desirable enhancement to any garden, but as few of us are blessed with natural ones, an increasing number of people are constructing their own.

There are three basic types:–
1 Concrete ponds – traditional method but somewhat laborious and expensive compared with more modern materials. Should still be considered when designing a raised or formal pond. Concrete, cement rendered bricks or blocks may still be the best materials where a hard wearing surface is required. This type of construction cannot be skimped: adequate footings and reinforcement will be required if cracking due to settlement is to be avoided. A good waterproofing agent should be used and any exposed surfaces of cement should be treated with Silglaze or similar to kill the lime.

2 Ready made – usually moulded fibreglass or plastic. The advantages are, apart from convenience, that these pools are very durable and relatively inexpensive. The disadvantages are that you are restricted in size and to a shape that was factory-designed. These are, however, ideal for installation into a patio, either sunken or raised.

3 Lined ponds – probably the most popular choice. Liners are available in varying price ranges. At the lower end, polythene is not sufficiently strong, is prone to damage and difficult to repair. Better quality liners such as butyl rubber or PVC are advisable and probably cheaper in the long run. They are flexible and easy to repair, and should last 20 years or more. Professional advice should be sought as to the best method of installation. To calculate the size of liner required, simply add twice the maximum depth to each of the maximum length and maximum width of the pool. Add one foot to each measurement for formal pools, due to the difficulty of positioning the liner exactly, and to allow for securing the edges.

The first thing to decide is where to site your pond. Apart from aesthetic considerations, it should be well away from trees, as falling leaves pollute the water, and out of the shadow of buildings. Whether the contours of the pool will be formal or informal will be determined by the site and personal preference. Either way, the ideal depth for an ornamental pool will be to have two thirds of the area 18 – 24" deep (in the middle), one third (all around the outside) forming a shelf 9 – 12" deep. Avoid sharp contours and islands.

Also, you may wish to have an electric pump to circulate and oxygenate the water, either in a fountain, cascade or both.

Eventually you will surely want to add fish. Avoid overcrowding, as too many will pollute their own environment. Please feed (sparingly) during the summer months. Provide an air hole in the winter ice. Thin ice may be broken gently by hand, but breaking thick ice can harm the fish. Instead, float a tennis ball on the surface to create a weak point, and pour warm water around it. Repeat during long periods of ice-up.

February (installation)
Avoid a windy day! For a liner pond:–

1 Mark out the shape with hose, string or sand.

2 Site level pegs outside the area as reference points when gauging depths and levels.

3 If aiming for the natural look, ensure sides slope between approx 45°.

4 Remove sharp objects.

5 Line level surfaces with 1" sand and slopes with old peat bags or polythene wrappings.

6 Position liner into shape, fill with a few gallons of water to hold in place.

7 Secure edge of liner with turfs or bricks whilst filling, frequently releasing pressure so that it pulls into shape – never allow it to stretch. Creases will not be noticeable when pond naturalises.

8 Trim off surplus liner when the pool is full.

9 Ensure edging is secure. If finishing with paving slabs, put a concrete footing around the edge for stability, before laying the liner, making sure this is level

For a pre-formed pond, the hole should be 12" larger than the pool to facilitate levelling, supporting the shelves and back filling. Backfill outside as the pond fills with water inside, to avoid distortion.

March
Expect visitors! Frogs and toads may well drop in for a little breeding. They are to be welcomed, as are the rarer newts. Look for the spawn. Most insects are also harmless, but watch out for diving beetles or water scorpion if you have small fish.

Arum Lily

Iris

April (planting)

Pond plants divide into four categories: submerged (foliage beneath water level) which compete with algaé for light and incrase oxygen levels – should eventually cover one third of the pool; lily-like (foliage floating on surface) which provide shade - beneficial to fish and inhibits algae; marginals (foliage above surface), grown for beauty and shade; and free floating. Lilies and free floaters should eventually cover half the surface.

Plant lillies in solid containers with garden soil (not compost) and a sachet of slow releasing fertiliser. They require alot of space. Marginals should be planted in baskets lined with hessian. Cover all containers with gravel to prevent fish disturbing soil. Introduce floaters in May.

Begin to feed fish sparingly – they lose appetite in cold spells.

May

A good time to stock with fish. Float bag containing fish in the water for 20 mins before releasing to equalise temparature. Treat water for parasites – it is vital that you know the capacity of your pond.

New ponds may develop grren algae – this is not unusual. An algicide may be used, but do not mix with other treatment.

Water lillies will reach surface late in the month. Introduce floaters.

Marsh Marigolds, musks and other marginals in full bloom.

June
Feed fish daily until autumn, taking care not to over feed – should be consumed within five minutes. Frantic activity amongst the marginals indicates they are breeding. Fry emerges in around three days, but eggs are often eaten – may be prudent to remove the roots carrying the eggs to a separate container.

Established lillies begin to flower. Irises at their best.

July
Healthy fish should be active, not gasping at surface. Decaying food or other matter can deplete oxygen. Fish gasping in the morning but improving during the day suggests that too much submerged plant life is absorbing oxygen during the night – thinning out will be beneficial. Fountains and cascades are advisable for oxygenation. Remove blanket weed by hand.

August
Lilies in full bloom – do not allow splash from fountain to fall on leaves. Remove decaying leaves. Never use inseticides on pond plants. Water snails are to be encouraged. Blue pickerel and arrowhead at their best.

September
Sweet garlingale, lobelia cardinalis and arum lily are at their best. When lifting and splitting established lilies, you will observe one mass of roots and tuber. Remove a few of the stronger 'breaks' by cutting through the tuber one inch either side. Trim off all foliage and re-pot, discarding at least 75% of redundant root and tuber. Leave fertilising with slow release sachet until spring.

Herons can raid at any time, but especially when garden is quieter. Trip wires may deter, but the only fully effective method is to net the pool completely.

October
Tidy foliage of marginals, trimming back over-vigorous growth to prevent a takeover. Remove dead foliage and if possible cover pool against autumn leaves falling. All pools gradually acquire a mulm of rotting material at the bottom, harbouring microscopic life which is of benefit to the pool. Only when it has reached such a depth that the pool is too shallow must one deal with it – every few years the pool should be emptied and throughly cleaned. Rigid pools should be refilled as quickly as possible, as sudden rains can cause them to float. Partial water changes are desirable, but treat water to neutralise chlorine and other harmful chemicals.

November
Non-hardy plants should be removed. For example, arum lily and lobelia cardinalis are best protected by planting (still in basket) into the garden and covering crowns with peat. Frosts will defoliate all plant life, but it will arise again in the spring.

Discontinue feeding fish. Remove fallen leaves. Make air holes in any ice (see above), remembering not to smash thick ice. A pool heater is the ideal solution.

LISKEARD WATER GARDENS

Bodgara Mill,
Pengover Road,
Liskeard.
Tel. (0579) 342278

There's much to commend a cool riverside walk on a summer's day, and few more beautiful settings in which to take one than the Seaton Valley. Be sure your route leads to these lovely water gardens, situated by the river and an important aquatics centre.

Established in 1985, the centre stocks a comprehensive range of cold water and tropical fish, housed in many aquaria, as well as aquatic plants and accessories. A range of books on the subject is for sale, and the owner is always ready to share her considerable knowledge, including advice on installing and landscaping your pond. She has also installed aquaria in doctors' surgeries and the like.

So, whether you are an enthusiastic amateur or seasoned veteran, a visit to this very agreeable site will pay dividends.

Open: 10am to 5pm Thurs - Sat, Tues & Weds by appointment only. Car park.

Swimming Pools

Nothing enhances a garden or house quite like a swimming pool; long regarded as a status symbol, the preserve only of the very wealthy, they are nevertheless fast growing in popularity, aided by a string of hot summers. Not only are they often pleasing to the eye, they provide unbeatable fun and healthy recreation for the boisterous young and arthritic old. And they may not be as expensive as you think.

In 1960 there were very few private pools in the country. Then various companies imported panel liner pools from America; waterproof structures supported in position by either concrete block walls or metal panels bolted together. The floor is screeded so that walls and floor provide a firm base on which the liner rests. Although quite inexpensive, the liner has a recommended life of only seven years, based on a five month annual season.

Costlier but virtually everlasting is the concrete tiled pool. The concrete is reinforced and rendered and tiled in mosaic, fixed with special adhesive and grout. Like the liner pool, it is fitted with high rate sand filters to keep the water clean, with chemicals, normally chlorine, being added. This kills bacteria which is then filtered out.

Given our climate, it is no surprise that indoor pools, although naturally the most expensive, are becoming especially more popular. However, this requires an air treatment plant to control humidity, particularly when the pool is used throughout the year.

Many accessories are available to help you maintain and enjoy your pool to the full: heaters, heat pumps, heat retention covers (manual or electric), counter current swimming devices, underwater lights, music, multisensory equipment, automatic pool cleaners, automatic dosing equipment to control chemical levels etc. As in other fields, new technology and the use of computers is eliminating manual chores.

Whichever format you choose, a swimming pool will enrich your leisure time and improve your fitness. In making such a major and important purchase, it is vital that you engage a company of proven reliability and expertise. A botched job will just leave you with a huge hole in the ground and your wallet!

Checklist

The Swimming Poll and Allied Trades Association (SPATA) is an association of swimming pool contractors whose members are all inspected and perform to a code of practice. The following is the SPATA checklist for prospective pool purchasers:–

1 Who are the parties to a contract and is the installer a SPATA member?

2 What is the method of construction and do you have detailed drawings and specifications?

3 Can the installer produce evidence of previous experience in this method of construction?

4 Can the pool be built in accordance with SPATA standards?

5 Can structural calculations for the pool shell be produced if required?

6 What, if any, are the risks specifically excluded from the contract? (eg high water table, excavation in rock, diversion of drains, water mains, electrical cables.)

7 What provision is made for dealing with external water pressure?

8 What is the warranty a) on the pool and b) ancillary equipment, and are there any limitations on use and emptying?

9 Do you understand the terms of payment?

10 What is the VAT liability?

11 Who will be responsible for after-sales maintenace and service?

12 Are any local planning consents required?

13 Who is responsible for site clearance and subsequent reinstatement?

14 Where is the plant to be housed? Is the housing waterproof and will there be any nuisance from noise or fumes?

15 Who is responsible for running services (gas, water, electric, drainage)) to the plant room? If this is the owner's responsibility, has the installer detailed exactly what is required?

16 What type of filter is to be fitted, what is the turnover rate, and what provision is made for the disposal of backwash water?

17 What type of heater is to be fitted and what is its capacity in relaion to a) pool surface area and b) pool water volume.

18 What method of water sterilisation and PH correction is proposed?

19 What is the proposed method of dealing with increased costs and extra works? No instructions involving variations and extra works should be given to the contractor's employees.

Before commencement on site

1 What is the exact location of the proposed pool agreed by all parties?

2 What is the finished level of the pool coping?

3 What is to be done with the excavated soil?

4 Is any covering and protection required for shrubs, lawns, drives, adjacent buildings etc?

5 What is the access route for site traffic?

6 Where are the materials to be unloaded and stored?

7 What is the route for cable and pipe trenches?

8 Where is the filter backwash to discharge?

Lawncare

The four years of drought are now just a memory, but those yellowing patches of dead, brittle grass were hardly worthy of the name 'lawn'. Almost miraculously it returns to a lush green at the first downpour of rain. This, plus its continual defiance of our best weeding efforts, tells us what a hardy plant is grass. Growing it is no problem; keeping it looking good is something else.

If starting from scratch, one must first decide what the lawn is for: is it mainly ornamental or will it have to take alot of wear and tear from children? Then, with a view to the appearance you require and the soil type in your garden, make your choice of grass. The chart on the next page may help.

The site may also need to be levelled - best done in summer - by raising low areas dug out from high ground. If your soil is a particularly heavy one, you would do well to dig in sand and peat. In the most severe cases of poor drainage you may have to consider installing a proper drainage system, either with a rubble-filled soakaway or by an arrangement of underground clay pipes.

Establishing the lawn
There are two ways of doing this: from seed or from turf. In either case the ground must be prepared about one month before.

1 Break up soil to depth of 6"–8", working in compost or manure.

2 Firm by walking on it and rake to an even surface.

3 Dress with general fertiliser.

4 If seeding, buy best mixture (without rye grass), preferably coated with bird-repellant. Sow late March to early June, or from early September to early October (avoid hot spells). Water well.

5 If turfing, best time is between November and March, so that roots may bond before dry weather. Stagger joints like brickwork,

leaving small gaps. Firm down turves lightly with spade. Sprinkle and rake mixture of soil, peat and sand over the surface. Water well.

GRASS TYPES

Soil	Conditions	Grass	Habit
Purpose: Play			
Heavy	Average/shady	Rough-stalked Meadow	Slightly creeping
Average/heavy	Average/sunny	Perennial rye/Timothy	Tall & tufted
Medium/light	Average/unshaded	Smooth-stalked Meadow	Creeping
Medium/light	Average/sunny	Creeping Red Fescue	Creeping
Medium/light	Any	Highland Bent	Tufted, creeping
Light	Average/sunny	Chewing's Fescue	Tufted, dwarf
Dry, chalky	Average/sunny	Crested Dog's Tail	Tufted, dwarf
Purpose: Leisure *(any of above may also be used)*			
Heavy, moist	Unshaded	Creeping Bent	Tufted, creeping
Any	Any	Annual Meadow	Tufted, dwarf
Purpose: Ornamental			
Average/acid	Average/shaded	Wavy Hair	Slightly tufted
Medium	Shaded	Wood Meadow	Slightly tufted

Mowers

For small lawns the old-fashioned push-me-pull-you cylinder mower is fine, but for larger ones a powered mower is advisable. It is a common mistake to buy too small – a false economy, as the mower's life will be shortened if over-extended. As a rule of thumb, Hayters offer the following advice: half tennis court, use 16"; between half and full size tennis court, use 18" or 19"; larger than this, use 21" and upwards.

Power is generated either by electricity or petrol engine. The former is not so popular, being less maneouverable and because of the danger of running over the cable. Rotaries are especially good for long and coarse grass and the hover mowers for banks.

Two key safety points to remember: many fingers have been lost of a result of attempts to remove grass blockages while blades are still rotating. This is easily done, as when the blades are moving quickly they cannot be seen. For extra safety, wear strong gloves. Toes are also vulnerable, so sturdy shoes are recommended.

Mowers should be overhauled at the end of a busy season, and the sump oil checked regularly. Keep blades sharp or there will be damage to your lawn. Store in cool, dry place away from children.

Mowing

1 For new lawns, adjust cutting height to between 1" and 1½". For established lawns, allow ½".

2 Cut every 7 to 10 days.

3 Do not cut when very wet.

4 If only light covering of clippings, these may be left. Otherwise they should be gathered up for the compost heap.

Maintaining your lawn

1. Feed during growing season. Many feeders also contain weedkiller and mosskiller. Follow instructions carefully, as an uneven spread can lead to scorching - best to use a proper dispenser.

2. Treat persistent weeds with spot killer or dig out by hand.

3. Treat moss with mosskiller, but you should try to eliminate root cause - could be poorly drained soil, weak grass, cutting too close or excessive use of roller when soil is wet.

4. In dry summers water regularly (in compliance with any local water restrictions, of course). Do not overwater - slow sprinklers desirable, and soak down to depth of about two inches. Evenings best, as fierce sun may lift water before it can properly soak.

5. Autumn is the busy time; once growing has ceased, lawns should be aerated by scouring with rake and punching holes with fork. Alternatively, use spiked roller.

6. This may be followed by topdressing with equal mix of peat, fine soil and sand. Feed one last time.

The Hayter's Lawncare Calendar reproduced here may serve as a prompt for year-round basic care.

LAWNCARE CALENDAR

JANUARY/FEBRUARY

If the weather is mild, occasionally cut the grass with the mower blades set high. Check equipment. Keep off the grass if frozen or waterlogged.

MARCH

Rake the grass thoroughly. Spike the lawn all over applying lawn sand if necessary. Keep mower blades high – just 'top' the grass.

APRIL

Re-seed bare patches, apply fertilisers and mosskiller towards the end of month. Mow regularly, lowering blades gradually.

MAY

Keep mowing, increasing the frequency as required. Treat with selective weed/feed preparations if you haven't fed the lawn in April.

JUNE

Mow lawns twice a week if possible working to a definite pattern. Water grass if necessary, remembering to soak thoroughly.

JULY

Treat grass with second application of fertiliser or weedkiller/fertiliser. Water in as necessary. Don't crop too closely.

AUGUST

Keep on mowing regularly and watering as necessary. Fill any cracks caused by drought with a mixture of sharp sand and soil.

SEPTEMBER

Raise mower blades and increase interval between mowings. Apply Autumn-Winter fertiliser, weedkiller and mosskiller.

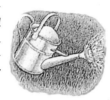

OCTOBER

Rake out thatch from turf and spike lawn to assist drainage. Brush in peat and sharp sand. Rake up dead leaves and twigs. Mow as necessary.

NOVEMBER

Use a stiff broom to remove wormcasts. Raise mower blades. Don't mow if very wet. Treat 'fairy rings' with fungicide.

DECEMBER

Rake all debris from lawns. Continue occasional cutting if weather is mild. Service your lawnmower and other equipment.

HANDY GARDEN MACHINERY
(at Kennedy's Garden Centre)
Hyde Road,
Kingsdown,
nr Swindon.
Tel. (0793) 721615
Fax (0793) 729988

Summary: competitive prices, expert advice, full back-up, comprehensive range (Hayter machines a speciality), some second hand. Open: 8am - 6pm Mon to Fri, 8:30am - 5pm Sat, 10am - 5pm Sun.

The new 'superstores' do offer low prices for garden machinery, but almost invariably lack range, service and, above all, expertise and back-up. Here at Handy's (a member of the Garden Machinery Association) you get the best of both worlds: prices which can often beat those of the superstores, plus, with 55 years trading behind them, an unsurpassed level of expert advice and after sales service. No less than 27 fully trained staff are familiar with all the leading brands, for which Handy's are agents. They are particularly strong on the HAYTER range, on which there are usually extra special offers.

But in 3,125 sq ft of showroom you will be spoilt for choice, from the smallest trimmer to the largest garden tractor, plus everything conceivable in between, including chainsaws and garden vacuuum cleaners. You could pick up a bargain second hand mower, always of good quality and thoroughly overhauled.

Deliveries can be made anywhere in the U.K., and customers (including a number of famous names) travel many miles, passing a superstore or two on the way, to avail themselves of one of the south of England's top dealers.

In addition to all this, there is of course the garden centre, which itself has much worth seeing, and a cafeteria.

JOHN MILLER (CORSHAM) Ltd

Bath Road, Chippenham.
Tel. (0249) 652573
Fax (0249) 443492

BY APPOINTMENT TO H R H
THE PRINCE OF WALES
SUPPLIERS OF GARDEN MACHINERY
AND CHAINSAWS

A Royal Warrant from the Prince of Wales is a rare accolade; the familiar plume of feathers mounted near the entrance to the showroom of John Miller (Corsham) Ltd tells its own story.

John Miller started the business in 1974 from his garden shed repairing garden machinery, progressing to rented premises in Corsham as trade increased. Success brought diversification and the need for larger and more modern premises. Thus in 1985 he moved to the present showroom, conveniently situated on the A4 Bath road, near the Pheasant roundabout.

The 2,000 sq ft showroom houses machinery ranging from push mowers to the most sophisticated ride-on mower; from hedge trimmers, chainsaws, generators, mountain bikes and all-terrain vehicles, to portable buildings, safety clothing and, of course, a full range of accessories. Naturally there's the backing of a full after sales service, including a comprehensive stores for most makes of machines.

Customers throughout the West Country come to John Millers for after sales service, for expert professional advice, and the repair, hire and maintenance service provided by John and his fully trained staff.

Open: Monday to Saturday 8:30am - 5:30pm (half-day Saturdays in winter). Agents for John Deer, Honda, Lawnflite, Flymo, Hayter, Atco. Delivery service.

CONSERVATION - COMPOSTING

One never ceases to wonder at the sheer volume of foliage which erupts during the growing season. Where does it all come from? Take some soil, add a little water and sunlight, and you have a seemingly tireless engine of growth which can produce anything from a daisy to a sequoia tree. This is most apparent during the autumn when one is trimming and tidying the garden, to be faced with the problem of disposing of it all. The obvious (and 'greenest') method is to return it to the ground, to provide sustenance for future growth. But it will, of course, have to be rendered into a usable state - composted.

When animals digest food they are, in a sense, composting. It's just enormously speeded up by enzymes. All organic material decays, but coarser matter should be shredded (see feature), otherwise it will take an inordinately long time. It must be said most gardeners just throw grass clippings and other assorted waste on to a heap. Far better is to construct a simple bin. This should be at least 3' square, with three walls of insulating material such as breeze blocks, timber or straw bales, built straight onto the soil so as to allow access for worms. The bottom layer should be of brushwood or similar to allow aeration. Add a variety of material (not just grass clippings), but never toxic waste or weeds which have seeded, and at the same time add in layers of a proprietary composter to accelerate bacterial action.

Perhaps the most convenient method is a rotating composter (see picture), which costs about £50 - £60. It is simply turned once a day and greatly speeds up the process. It has the advantage of being movable, and a wheelbarrow is easily filled from it.

Your garden will benefit noticably from a steady addition of organic material, and of course it also helps the soil retain water.

LOWES MOWER SHOP Ltd

Stewart's Garden-Lands, Lyndhurst Road, Somerford, nr Christchurch.
Tel. (0425) 278820
Fax (0425) 278860

The many attractions of Garden-Lands have been described on another page, but special mention must go to this long-established and highly reputable garden machinery company, with a 2,800 sq ft showroom on the site.

Founded in 1948, the business retains good old-fashioned personal service but is also bang up-to-date with the latest technology. Managing Director Dave Tyler and colleague Peter Shearing (who's been with Lowes since 1956 and is an acknowledged expert on garden machinery) take pride in their expertise, and are founder members of a new professional body, 'Lawn Leaders.' Few other retailers can match their level of back up and sound advice, which should be considered indispensable in what is, after all, quite a major purchase.

Prices are most competitive, and all types and sizes of mowers are stocked (agents for Flymo, Qualcast, Atco, Mountfield, Hayter, Alko, Husqvarna), as well as trimmers, chainsaws and, increasingly in vogue, shredders (pictured). These can render the toughest branches into small chips within seconds, ready for composting; 'eco-friendly' and a real boon to the gardener. With 15 models, Lowes claim to have the widest range in the South of England.

The showroom itself is bright and pleasant, with a glass roof and laid out with plants and shrubs. There's a full range of accessories and of course an efficient repair service.

SPECIAL NOTE: DELIVERY ANYWHERE IN THE U.K., CARRIAGE PAID.

Open: Mon to Sat 9am - 6pm (8pm Fridays in summer), Sundays 10am - 6pm.

Seed Propagation

Checklist

General hint: store seeds in cool, dark place – fridge is ideal!

In the open

1 Resist the temptation to sow too early, during a warm spell in January or February, for instance. When hedgerows start to leaf, that is one good indicator. Wait until frosts are over before sewing half-hardy annuals, perennials and the more delicate vegetables.

2 Prepare soil by breaking up into fine tilth, removing stones and levelling.

3 Dust with general garden fertiliser.

4 Sow seeds thinly to avoid waste and hard work later on thinning them out.

5 Water well and maintain a watering programme.

6 If sowing vegetables (or indeed annuals in some cases), form a drill of even depth and water before sewing. Gently push back soil to cover.

7 Cover with nets to protect from birds.

Under glass

1 Fill tray with seeding compost, level and firm.

2 Water using fine rose on can.

3 Make holes for larger seeds, insert seeds, cover to depth of seed.

4 Fine seeds are best put on piece of white paper which is then folded to form a chute. Such seeds will require little or no covering with compost.

5 More difficult seeds should be 'roughed up' a little (with emery paper or similar) to assist penetration by water.

6 Place glass or clear polythene over tray.

7 Protect from extremes of temperature – do not leave exposed to full sun.

8 As soon as seedlings emerge, remove glass or polythene and place trays in full light.

9 Keep them moist, always using fine rose.

10 Prick out seedlings before they become overcrowded.

11 Do not plant out into garden until you are quite certain there will be no more frosts!

Stock is easy to grow and is sweetly fragrant

Pinks are easily grown from seed.

Lupins propagate readily and like seaside areas.

Poison Plants Checklist
If you have young children, it is as well to be aware of the following:–

Trees
laburnum, yew tree needles and seeds.

Shrubs
black bryony, box, brooms, buckthorn, cherry laurel, daphne mezereum, hawthorn, ivy, mistletoe, mock orange, oleander, privet, rhododendron, snowberry, all spurges, white bryony, wisteria.

Flowering plants
baneberry, black nightshade, buttercup, columbine, cowbane, dog's mercury, deadly nightshade, dropwort (tubular, hemlock, fine leaved), fool's parsley, foxglove, fritillary, green hellebore, hemlock, henbane, lily of the valley, meadow saffron, monkshade.

Other Safety Ideas
1 Turn ponds into sandpits – or at least cover securely. If you must have water, how about a bubbling fountain?

2 Avoid prickly bushes, like roses or holly.

3 Protect sharp corners on brickwork etc.

4 Shield lower panes of greenhouse and glass frames.

5 Avoid ornamental gravel – children swallow it and cats relieve themselves in it.

6 Do not place swings etc on hard surfaces, slopes or near overhanging branches. Ensure play equipment cannot topple.

7 Keep play area visible from house.

8 Prevent access to road.

Beautiful but deadly, Mock Orange

Growing Roses in the West Country

Rosa Mundi

Photos courtesy of Peter Beales

Blanc Double de Coubert

With literally thousands of varieties of rose available, choosing those best suited for one's own requirements is a daunting task. So many factors must be considered; not only the obvious, such as size, colour or perfume, but also the soil type and climate.

The vast majority of varieties tolerate our conditions in the South West, indeed some are ideally suited. However, there are a few, like the old-fashioned teas and many of the Chinas, which will struggle in the colder areas "up country," unless they can be found a very sheltered position. Alternatively, they may be grown outside in an ornamental tub during summer, to be brought indoors for winter.

The RUGOSA roses make ideal hedging plants. They are tough, relatively free-flowering and in many cases will provide a beautiful display of hips in the autumn. SCABROSA is just one of this group. It bears large, single, deep pink flowers throughout the summer, followed by magnificent tomato-like hips. Another attribute is the autumn colouring of the leaves, which become a true golden yellow. FRU DAGMAR HASTRUP and BLANC DOUBLE DE COUBERT are also equally worthy of garden space, although the latter does not have the hip-bearing qualities of the other two.

Some delightfully perfumed varieties can be found amongst the ranks of the GALLICA roses, which flower in profusion in June. This group is also very strong and hardy. ROSA MUNDI is one of the oldest of these, and is reputedly named after Fair Rosamund, mistress of Henry II. It has semi double blooms which are striped with carmine and white. ROSA GALLICA OFFICINALIS makes a good companion to Rosa Mundi, being identical in growth but with pure deep pink flowers.

Scabrosa hips

In very windy areas shorter varieties are easier to cope with. One of the best procumbent (ground cover) roses is BONICA. It is of open, lax habit, extremely healthy, and bears masses of open, pink flowers throughout the summer months. There are many low-growing varieties, but to add to the scope of colour the BELLS group is recommended. Again, they are of a healthy disposition but are denser in habit than Bonica. If grown together the red, pink and white Bells make a wonderful display.

Old fashioned rambling and scrambling roses create a spectacle in mid-summer and may be considered for a number of uses: many are vigorous enough to obliterate a garden shed or reach the highest branches of tall trees, where they produce trusses of dainty flowers. One such is RAMBLING RECTOR, a very old variety which is also sometimes thought to be Shakespeare's Musk. Its creamy white flowers will nod in clusters at up to heights of around 20 feet. KIFTSGATE is yet more vigorous, and can reach 30 feet with ease. Smaller varieties can be trained over arches and against trellises. BLUSH NOISETTE is one of the hardier of the Noisette family. Although less vigorous than many, it will produce flowers of pale lilac pink repeatedly throughout the season.

Some of the Multiflora Ramblers are also repeat-flowering, namely GHISLAINE DE FELIGONDE and PHYLIS BIDE. Both bear peach-coloured flowers, although the latter is also tinged with pink and yellow. Ghislaine is likely to reach a height a little lower than Phyllis, but they will end up somewhere between eight and ten feet.

In exposed areas wind is the big problem. It is sad to see roses broken off at ground level and standard roses snapped off just below beautiful flowering heads. Deep planting will help ensure stability. The union (the point at which stem and roots join) should be about one inch below ground level. This depth of planting also helps maintain moisture during the dry summers such as we have experienced in recent years.

Standard roses should be well staked, with two or three ties along the length of the stem. It is wise to stake the standard at time of planting, as doing so later may well damage roots, causing unneccessary suckering.

To help prevent wind rock in winter, modern rose bushes can be partially pruned in the autumn. Reduce their height to between one third and one half, ensuring that all cuts are made at an angle to prevent water settling on the wound. The final prune can take place in spring as usual.

Soil preparation is of great importance before planting roses. The addition of well-rotted farmyard manure is beneficial both nutritionally and structurally. Ensure that it is well dug-in and not just put in the bottom of the hole, as this can cause scorching. If manure is not available, a mixture of peat and bone meal is as beneficial.

In pollution-free areas blackspot and other airborne diseases can be rife. As with all disease, prevention is better than cure, so a spraying programme is advisable. Start before any sign of trouble appears and continue every other week until leaf fall is imminent. Chemicals are available which deal with several different diseases and insects at the same time. Obviously, they make for an easier life. It is wise, however, to alternate the chemical used, as resistance will build-up to continual use of the same kind.

Whilst good husbandry is the key to beautiful roses, a few blemishes can easily be forgiven. A flower is just as lovely whether or not the bush has a touch of mildew or blackspot.

Bonica

Photos courtesy of Peter Beales

Planting Container Roses

Roses prefer clay soils and locations which receive direct sunlight for at least part of the day. Using container-grown roses, results as good as clay can be achieved in any soil provided that some simple rules are observed:-

1. Check the acidity of the soil. If it is below pH 6.3 lime should be added.

2. For each rose plant dig a hole about 12 inches deep and 15 inches across. Place the top soil to one side.

3. Place sufficient well-rotted or proprietary compost in the bottom of the hole to allow the top of container-grown roots to be three inches below soil level when placed upon the compost.

4. Surround the plant rooting system with added compost. Cover the root plug and composted area with top soil. Water in.

5. Prune in March each year.

Fertiliser

Rose plants require a level dessertspoonful (or heaped teaspoonful) of fertiliser containing 20% nitrogen, 10% phosphate and 10% potash, or the equivalent. Feed in early March, and again in June, of each year.

Pests and Diseases

Fungus diseases are more prevalent in areas where the air does not circulate freely, so encouraging high humidity. Try to avoid planting in unventilated positions (such as under hedges). Hold climbers away from walls (using trellis, for example) to improve ventilation.

Control

Use general garden spray such as ROSECLEAR. Preventative spraying every 14 days, seven days where outbreak has occurred. Occasionally downy mildew becomes established to a degree where it fails to respond, in which case specialist advice should be sought.

Disease or pest	Symptoms
Powdery mildew:	whitish powdery deposit on new growth
Downy mildew:	some leaves successively turn yellow with purple-brown patches subsequently dropping off. A total yellowing is more likely due to lack of water.
Blackspot:	Large round black spots on leaves, starting at lower levels. Leaves do not usually turn yellow.
Green aphid & red spider:	troublesome little devils!

American Pillar Rose

Camellias in the West Country

by Jennifer Trehane of Trehane Nursery, Hampreston, near Wimborne.

West Country soils range from the totally unsuitable (alkaline chalk downland) to the ideal (acid sandy or peaty heathland) as far as camellias are concerned. In between, particularly in the river valleys, are soils which are more neutral and of a loamier texture.

Camellias are shrubs which seem to provoke strong feelings and a determined spirit in those who have unsuitable soils, and there are many who have good collections in tubs, pots and in specially-constructed raised beds, lined with polythene and filled with an ericaceous compost. The beauty of container growing is the flexibility: the tubs can be moved around to ensure that the plants are in the best position outdoors in the summer months, and brough in to a glasshouse or conservatory (never the dry, centrally-heated atmosphere of a modern house) for the winter. Many growers do this because they get the full benefit of the flowers and to protect the roots, easily killed if frozen, from frost. Varieties of compact habit such as Anticipation, which is wonderfully free-flowering with rich rose peony-form flowers. The red Dr Burnside and the red and white striped Betty Foy Sanders are also good. There are many more and it is worth considering white-flowered varieties, which damage so easily in bad weather outdoors but are glorious under glass. Matterhorn, with its pure, glistening white formal double blooms and extra glossy green leaves, or Lily Ponds, with long, almost tubular petals, are both rewarding.

Scented camellias are becoming widely known as more and more people realise what a joy they are, as many flower in the dull, dreary days from October to January. Some of these gems will flower outdoors in really mild sheltered gardens in the South West, particularly in Cornwall, but most are happier in the warmth of a consevatory. Hugh Evans, Rainbow and Tanya flower in the autumn. Spring Mist, which can also be grown in a conservatory hanging basket, flowers from January to April, while Fragrant Pink starts a little later. Both have lovely bronze young growth outdoors. In the garden, camellias of all sorts and sizes will thrive if the soil is acid and free-draining, and has plenty of organic matter, such as peat or leafmould, incorporated into it at planting. The light intensity, particularly in the coastal areas, is quite strong, so some shade is needed for most varieties, otherwise leaves become dull and tend to look unhappy. Shelter from severe wind is an advantage, especially cold winter easterlies. Adequate water is necessary, especially during the July to Octber period when flower buds are forming for the following season. Add a 2oz to-the-square-yard helping of an azalea/rhododendron fertiliser in April and again in July to keep the plants healthy. Really old, very well rotted farmyard manure can be used at planting, but fresher manure will kill the roots of most camellias, as will strong animal-based fertilisers later on.

For those who live in the really mild microclimates, the choice of camellias is huge, and even some of the rare species from China can be tried. C. grijsi, with its small white scented flowers, C. tsaii, which has a lovely graceful habit and small white flowers, C. yuhsienensis and many more are worth considering. The tea plant, C. sinensis, is fun to try, but be prepared for some browning at the tips of the leaves in early spring.

Camellias are relatively free from pests and diseases. Probably the most common is 'sooty mould', which makes an unsightly mess on the upper surface of the leaves. The cause is traced to insect feeding - mostly scale insects which suck the sap from the underside of the leaves and drop their excreta (honeydew) on to the leaves below, making an ideal base for the sooty mould fungus. Kill the insects first, using an insecticide such as Sybol or Tumblebug. Then either wipe off the mould with a damp sponge or use a fungicide such as Nimrod T. You may have to repeat sprayings.

With the great increase in popularity of camellias in recent years, there is one possible concern for the future: that is the fact that many varieties will grow to be far too big for their gardens. This can be avoided by snipping back each year in order to keep things under control. Annual pruning in this way does not inhibit

flowering too much; a gigantic bush which has to be severely chopped back will grow again, but may not be able to flower for a couple of years.

Camellias are such rewarding shrubs, and far better tempered than most people realise. It's no wonder that we in the West Country, making the most of our fortunate climate, have probably more camellias in our gardens than any other part of the country.

Your Soil - Alkaline or Acid?

Hard tap water is one indicator of alkaline areas. Acid soil occurs in many town gardens, and where the soil is sandy or peaty.

But there are many different types of topsoil, as indicated by the map opposite. To be quite sure of your own soil, use a soil-testing kit. Application of hydrated lime will increase alkalinity, peat increases acidity.

Plants for alkaline soil

Name	Height	Description
Hedge Maple	15 – 20'	good autumn colour
Crab Apple	10 – 20'	spring blossom, autumn fruits
Barberry	4 – 8'	orange–yellow flowers in spring, purple/red fruits, autumn colour
Cornelian Cherry	8 – 12'	yellow flowers Feb – April, red fruits later
Spindle tree	6 – 10'	rich autumn colour, poison fruits
Mock Orange	6 – 9'	heavily perfumed flowers
Aubretia (perennial)	3 – 4"	shades of purple in spring
Clematis (climber)	– 40'	many shades, spring/summer
Gypsophila (perennial)	2 – 3'	small white flowers, June – Aug (ideal for sprays)
Daffodil	2 – 3'	yellow/white flowers in spring
Black-eyed Susan (perennial)	1 – 3'	Bright yellow flowers July – Oct
Pansy (perennial)	2 – 10"	full range of colours, April –Aug

Plants for acid soil

Name	Height	Description
Holly	10 – 25'	evergreen, berries in winter
False Acacia	20 – 30'	cream flowers in June, pale leaves
Barberry	4 – 8'	orange-yellow flowers in spring, purple/red fruits, autumn colour
Rock Rose	4 – 6'	pink or white flowers, May/June
Bell Heather	9 – 12"	white/pink flowers, Jun – Oct
Spanish Gorse	2 – 4'	gold flowers June/July
Japonica	4 – 6'	orange-yellow flowers, April/May
Tamariscifolia	2½'	low growing spreading conifer
Honeysuckle (climber)	15 – 20'	scented yellow flowers, July/Aug
Sea Holly (perennial)	12 – 18"	blue flowers Jul/Sept, silver leaves
Red Hot Poker (peren)	2 – 5'	flame orange flowers, Jun/Oct
London Pride (peren)	1'	pink flowers in May, thick leaves
Rhododendrons, Azaleas, Camellias – huge variety of sizes and colours		

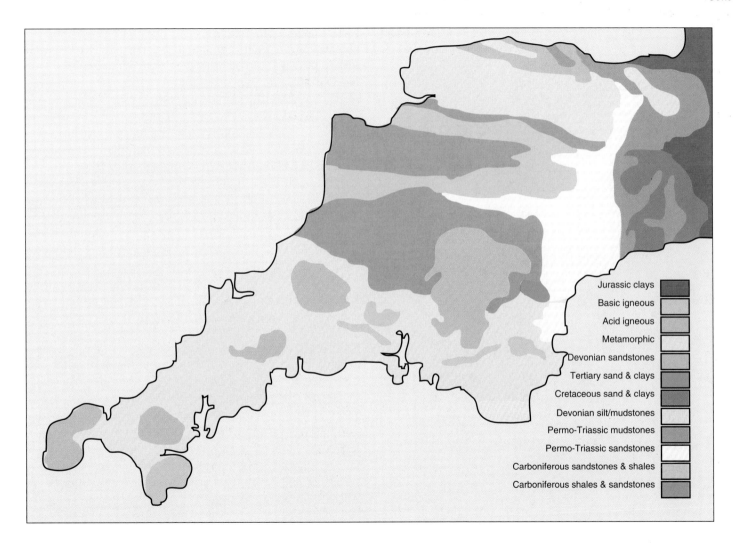

Jurassic clays
Basic igneous
Acid igneous
Metamorphic
Devonian sandstones
Tertiary sand & clays
Cretaceous sand & clays
Devonian silt/mudstones
Permo-Triassic mudstones
Permo-Triassic sandstones
Carboniferous sandstones & shales
Carboniferous shales & sandstones

The Variety of the West Country

by Peter Killen O.N.D. of Robin Hill Landscapes, Bournemouth.

The South West offers a wealth of landscapes. The keen gardener who wishes to cultivate a garden with exotics will live in one of the many valleys mostly along the south coast or open to the effects of the Gulf Stream. These micro-climates enable one to grow many imports from the antipodes, such as Dixons Palm and other temperate/sub tropicals.

The ideal valley will have a natural stream or river flowing through, which can be diverted to create wondrous waterfalls, pools, grottos with ferns bristling from dark crevices dripping with mosses and glaucous blue lichen. One can also create smaller versions in most gardens, however humble. The majority of gardens have exposed sites which need to be protected by windbreaks such as a trellis or lattice fencing, or woodland breaks, for which some grants may be obtained, or simple hedging, which may need to be salt-tolerant near the coast - Griselina, Escallonia etc, Tamarix on sandy northern coasts.

The soil conditions vary enormously even within a few miles: the chalk hills of Wiltshire yield to the acid sands of the New Forest and East Dorset, which allow the Ericaceous plants to flourish, such as heathers, rhododendrons, camellias etc. In mid and west Dorset we are back into chalk hills, with Weymouth ending in a sticky, heavy clay. The Somerset Levels offer an intriguing place for planting, whereas the edge of the moors through Exmoor, Dartmoor and Bodmin Moor, and mid-Cornwall, are severely exposed, with small pockets of refuge for the determined gardener to form his personal stamp on the landscape.

The South West is one of the prime areas of England for gardens of great interest, offering challenges which may in the first place be overcome by good design and use of sympathetic materials, followed by the crowning of plants, and for the daring the vast variety of half-hardy trees and shrubs available from the many specialist nurseries.

Landscaping your Garden in the West Country

by Helen Mason of Endsleigh Landscapes,
Endsleigh Garden Centre, Ivybridge.

"Landscaping? I can't possibly afford to have that done, it's too expensive!"

That is a common but mistaken impression, sometimes aided by the media which, while showing how worthwhile an investment is landscaping, may misleadingly quote extravagant fees charged for the work. The industry is trying to address the misconception, pointing out that a small outlay can often produce pleasing results. Domestic landscaping is split into several areas; it is perhaps a case of 'pick and mix' to achieve the right combination to suit customers' requirements. It is definitely not a case of bulldozing the whole garden and costing a small fortune!

But why is it worth landscaping? Reasons vary: the garden may just need tidying, adding an extra room to the house, as it were, and increasing its value; or to  provide a design from which to work over a long period of time as the garden becomes more established. These are just two examples, but whether yours is a 'pocket handkerchief' or a three-acre spread, the service may be beneficial to you.

Design is perhaps the aspect which proves most invaluable. This provides a base on which to build, containing all your requirements, in sympathy with the surrounds, yet both functional and attractive. You can work from the design at your own pace - the actual construction or planting need not take place all at once, and a few years may elapse before the final results, but at least you will have an ultimate goal for which to aim.

The other design service that will save a lot of heartache in the long run is the planting plan. The impulse to over plant ("Isn't that pretty - that would go well next to ...) is an understandable one, but plants that are not suitable for the conditions, or which are destined to grow into monstrosities which swamp everything else, are best avoided. With a plan, shrubs and herbaceous plants to fill a border can be bought over a period of time, spreading the expense.

Design or planting plans can be 'D.I.Y.', or a landscape contractor can carry out as much or as little of the work as you wish. It is worthwhile employing only  reputable contractors - repair bills can be expensive! A much maligned industry, landscaping is seen too much as only for the wealthy, but in fact there are many excellent services for those on a limited budget.

Lilium tigrinum

Arbutus unedo

The West Country is known for its lovely cottage gardens, and if you would like to emulate them, and establish a garden of all-year-round colour, follow Helen Mason's calendar tips:-

January/ February	**Cornus alba 'Elegantissima'** - red stems **Ilex 'Silver Queen'** - cream/green variegated foliage **Leymus arenarius** - blue/grey leaves
March	**Euphorbia amygdaloides 'Purpurea'** - tiny yellow flowers with red leaf bracts **Spiraea thunbergii** - white flowers
April	**Cytisus x kewensis** - slightly scented cream/yellow flowers **Forsythia tremonia** - yellow flowers **Lewisia** - pink herbaceous perennials
May	**Caenothus 'Dignity'** - scented powder blue flowers, also a flush in September **Centaurea montana 'Alba'** - white thistle-like flowers **Lonicera periclynenum 'Belgica'** - scented red flowers **Rosmarinus prostrata** - blue flowers, scented foliage
June	**Alchemilla mollis** - tiny sulphur yellow flowers **Cistus 'Silver Pink'** - dog rose pink flowers which last only one day, but profuse **Crocosmia 'Lucifer'** - red flowers **Erigeron speciosus** - pink herbaceous annuals **Philadelphus coronarius 'Aureus'** - white scented flowers, yellow foliage
July	**Buddleia 'Black Knight'** - dark purple scented flowers **Hebe 'Purple Queen'** - violet flowers, purple foliage **Lavendula 'Hidcote'** - pale pink flowers, scented grey foliage **Olearia macrodonta** - tiny white scented daisy-like flowers
August	**Alcaea** - mixed colours, from yellow, white pink, red **Clematis tangutica** - yellow lantern flowers **Lilium tigrinum** - orange spotted flowers **Lychnis coronaria** - deep pink flowers, grey foliage
September	**Nepeta mussinii** - lavender/blue flowers, grey green scented foliage **Pyracantha 'Orange Glow'** - orange berries **Sedum spectabilis 'Brilliant'** - carmine pink flowers
October	**Arbutus unedo (Strawberry Tree)** - clusters of white flowers (like Lily of the Valley), red strawberry-like fruits **Caryopteris x clandonensis 'Heavenly Blue'** - deep cornflower-blue flowers
November	**Tricyrtis hirta** - milk/white with pink/red spotted flowers
December	**Viburnum bodnantense 'Dawn'** - pink scented flowers

Erigeron speciosus

ROBIN HILL LANDSCAPES

162 Pine Road, Winton, Bournemouth.
Tel. (0202) 525676
Fax (0202) 536745

Peter Killen is widely acknowledged as one of Britain's most accomplished landscape gardeners. Still only 39, he has been managing director of Robin Hill, first established in 1946, since 1978, and is also currently Honorary Secretary of BALI (British Association of Landscape Industries), the only national body representing the industry. He has also taught the subject, and numbers Roddy Llewellyn amongst his former pupils.

Six gardeners work for him, and the diversity of work they do, and the depth of knowledge required to do it, would amaze most people. Starting with design, and in addition to a comprehensive understanding of plants, there may also be a call for architectural and engineering skills in the construction of walls, for example, or watergardens, terraces and pavings. Not averse to using a computer, Peter Killen nevertheless maintains that it is the 'human ingredient' which is most important.

A speciality of the company is in fitting extra space into small or steeply sloping gardens by the use of retaining walls in timber, stone, or raised patios in the form of timber decks, all of which have a long life span. As the photo shows, this can be most effective with a pond to the front, fed by a little waterfall, so that the deck forms a bridge. It can work for you, whether your garden is large or small, and modern techniques employed by Peter Killen improve quality but keep to a modest cost.

Customers have ranged from owners of the most modest suburban plot to huge country estates; all projects are seen as enjoyable and challenging. The eye can be deceived into seeing a small garden as larger than it is, and a large garden can be compartmentalised to make it much more intriguing and mysterious. Why settle for the ordinary when you could easily have the breathtaking?

Working hours are from 8am to 5pm Monday to Friday. Visitors by appointment only. Design only commissions are undertaken - can be handled by post.

Trees

For seaside areas

Acer plantanoides (Norway Maple)

Fraxinus excelsior (Common Ash)

Acer pseudoplantus (Sycamore)

Picea omorika (Serbian Spruce)

Alnus incana (Grey Alder)

Pines (Scots, Corsican, Austrian)

Betula (Birch)

Populus alba

Castina sativa (Sweet Chestnut)

Populus candicans Aurora (Poplar)

Crategus (Flowering Thorn)

Sorbus aria (Whitebeam)

Cupressocyparis leylandii

Sorbus aucuparia (Rowan)

For chalky soils

Acer	Malus
Betula	Populus
Carpinus	Prunus
Catalpa	Pyrus
Crataegus	Robinia
Fagus	Salix
Gleditsia	Sorbus
Laburnum	

Poplars

Laburnum

For badly drained soil
Acer negundo (Ash-leafed Maple)
Fraxinus
Alnus (Alder)
Liquidamber styraciflua (Sweet Gum)
Amelancher canadensis (Snowy Mesipilis)
Liriodendron tulipfera (Tulip Tree)
Betula pendula (Silver Birch)
Populus
Carpinus
Sorbus aucuparia (Mountain Ash)
Crataegus
Weeping Silver Pear
Willow

For exposed sites
Acer (Maples)
Laburnum vossii (Golden Rain Tree)
Betula (Birch)
Populus
Carpinus betulus (Hornbeam)
Quercus (Oak)
Crataegus (Flowering Thorn)
Sorbus aucuparia
Fagus sylvatica (Green Beech)
Sorbus aria (Whitebeam)
Fraxinus excelsior (Common Ash)
Tilia (Limes)

Flowering Trees
Aesculus (Horse Chestnut)
Malus (Crab Apples)
Catalpa bignioides (Indian Bean Tree)
Prunus (Cherry)
Cotoneaster
Snowy Mesipilus
Crataegus
Sorbus (Rowans or Whitebeams)
Laburnum vossii
Japanese varieties (Kanzan, Sakura,
Amanogawa, Pink Perfection)

Trees with coloured leaves
Acers
Poplar (tinged white)
Eucalyptus gunnii (silver-blue)
Prunus (Plum)
Fagus (Beech - purple)
Robinia (golden yellow)
Golden Ash
Weeping Silver Lime
Golden Honey Locust Tree
Weeping Silver Pear
Malus (Crab Apple - bronze)
Whitebeam (green & silver)

Crab Apple

More unusual trees
Ailianthus altissima (Tree of Heaven)
Huge leaves, 30'.
Betula dalecarlica (Swedish Beech)
Fine leaves, 25'
Catalpa bignonioides (Indian Bean Tree)
Heart-shaped leaves, 18'
Davida involucrata (Handkerchief Tree)
Large bright leaves, 15'
Fagus (Beech), Weeping or Purple
Cascading stems, 15-18'
Liriodendron tulipfera (Tulip Tree)
4-lobed leaves, 35'
Northofagus (Antarctic Beech)
Tiny, shiny leaves, 18'
Paulownia tomentosa
Long leaves, mauve flowers, 15'
Zelkovia serrata
Toothed, rounded leaves, 15-18'

Trees for small gardens
Betula youngii (Weeping Birch)15'
Cotoneaster hybridus Pendulus 6 - 12'
Malus (Crab Apples) 15-18', many varieties
Prunus (Flowering Cherry) 15', Amanogawa, Sakura
Weeping Pussy Willow 6-10'
American Weeping Willow 15'

Flowering Cherry

Shrubs

For seaside areas

Arbutus Unedo
  (strawberry tree)
Choisya Ternata
Cordyline
Cotoneaster
Cytisus
Eleagnus
Escallonia
Euonymous
Fuchsia
Garrya Elliptica
Genista
Hebe
Hydrangeas Macrophylla

Ilex Aquifoloium
Lavendula
Olearea
Pittosporum
Pyracantha
Rosmarinus
Santolina
Senecio
Spartium
Spiraea
Tamarix
Viburnum
Yucca

For chalky soils

Arbutus
Aucuba
Berberis
Buddleia
Buxus
Ceanothus
Choisya
Cistus
Cornus Mas
Corytus

Kolkwitzia
Lavendula
Ligustrum
Olearia
Philadelphus
Photinia
Pittosporum
Pyracantha
Rhus
Ribes

Fuchsia

Yucca

Chalky soils (continued)

Cotoneaster

Deutzia

Eleagnus

Escallonia

Eunymous

Forsythia

Fuchsia

Garrya

Hebe

Hypericum

Ilex

Kerria

Rosmarinus

Sambucus

Santolina

Senecio

Spartium

Symphoricarpus

Syringa

Tamarix

Vinca

Weigela

Yucca

For clay soils

Aucuba Japonica

Berberis Species

Chaenomeles Species

Choisya Ternata

Cornus Species

Corylus Species

Cotoneaster Species

Forsythia Species

Hypericum Species

Mahonia Species

Philadelphus Species

Potentilla Species

Ribes Sanguineum

Skimmia Japonica

Spiraea Species

Symphoricarpus Species

Viburnum Species

Vinca Species

Wegela Species

For the rockery

Acer japonicum Aureum
Acer palmatum Dissectum
Acer palmatum Dissectum
Atropurpureum

Berberis thunbergii
Atropurprueum Nana

Erica Species
Hebe Armstrongii
Hebe Carl Teschner

Hebe pinguifolia Pagei

For heavy shade

Aucuba japonica
Common Box
Camellias
Eleagnus eddingei
Eleagnus pungens Maculata
Lingustrum Species
Baggins Gold Honeysuckle
Mahonia aquifolium

Japanese Spurge
Common Laurel
Skimmia japonica Foremanii
(female)

Skimmia japonica Rubella
(male)

Symphoricarpus Species
Viburnum davidii
Vinca Species

For ground cover

Berberis thunbergii
Atropurperea Nana

Cotoneaster Coral Beaut
Cotoneaster danmeri
Cotoneaster horizontalis Variegata
Cotoneaster salicifolius
Cotoneaster salicifolius Repens
Euonymus fortunei Emerald & Gold
Euonymus fortunei & Gaiety
Euonymus fortunei Variegatus

Gaultheria procumbens
Hebe Carl Teschner
Hebe pinguifolia Pagei
Hedera Ivy
Hypericum calycinum
Japanese Spurge
Vinca major Common
Periwinkle

Vinca minor Variegata

Climbing Rose

For exposed sites

Berberis
Buddleia
Chaenomeles
Cornus
Corylus
Cotoneaster
Deutzia
Eleagnus pungens Maculata Aurea
Euonymous japonicus
Ilex
Kerria
Tamarix

Pernettya
Philadelphus (Mock Orange)
Philadelphus Virginal
Potentilla
Rhododendrons
Roses
Salix (Willow)
Sambucus nigra (Elder)
Spiraea
Symphoricarpus Magic Berry
Ulex europaeus Plenus
Viburnum

For wet sites

Arundinaria
Cornus (Dogwood)
Cornus mas (Cornelian Cherry)
Pernettya
Philadelphus (Mock Orange)
Rhododendrons

Salix (Willow)
Sambucus nigra (Elder)
Spiraea
Symphoricarpus Magic Berry
Viburnum - deciduous forms
(Opulus, Sterile,
Xanthocarpum, Lantana)

Rhododendron

Palm reading

by Tim Eley of Torbay Palms, Coffinswell, nr Newton Abbot.

"The English Riviera" lays claim to this epithet largely on the back of its own Torbay Palm, which graces the seafront and gardens of the area. Palms are grown in other parts of the country, but nowhere other than the West Country, with its mild, frost-free winters, can boast such abundance and diversity.

In fact, the Torbay Palm (Cordyline australis or Dracaena Palm) originates from New Zealand, and was introduced to this country in 1820. Once classified in the Liliaceae family, it now belongs to the Agaveacae and is, in fact, not a true palm. Quite hardy, it grows outdoors up to a height of 10 to 15ft, less if kept in a pot, and tolerates salt winds. It flowers after eight to ten years, bearing plume-like panicles up to three feet long by two feet wide, of fragrant cream-white flowers. Four varieties are now available: the ever popular **Green Torbay Palm**; the **Torbay Red**; **Sundance**, with a deep red vein in the centre of a dark green leaf; and **Torbay Dazzler**, a beautiful plant with green and creamy white striped sword-like leaves, the centre vein becoming salmon pink at the base.

New techniques in tissue culture mean that ever more varieties can be readily developed. Those in the pipeline for 1994 include **Torbay Surprise** (variegated yellow/green), **Torbay Wide** (extra wide green leaf) and **Torbay Sunset** (green leaf with deep red vein). Also on the way is a variegated red variety.

Planting and maintenance

Palms should be planted in well drained soil in a sunny, sheltered spot, and peat added when planting. They should be kept well watered until established, and fed every two to three weeks from April to September with a general fertiliser. Reckon that leaf volume will double each year. They make excellent patio plants, but of course planting in tubs will limit growth.

Propagation

Take 1½" cutting off the root and plant UPSIDE DOWN in multipurpose compost. Grow under glass for at least 12 months.

Seeds should be sown in seed compost in April at temperature of 16-18°c.

More exotic palms

True palms can and are grown in the area: **Trachycarpus fortunei**, more commonly known as Chusan or Chinese Windmill Palm, is hardy, slow-growing and endowed with a very hairy stem; **Chamaerops humilis** (European Fan Palm) is also quite common, as is **Phoenix canariensis** (Canary Island Date Palm).

The following, although rarer, can also survive temperatures of -8°c or even lower:-

Butia	Jubaea
Livistona australis	Sabal minor
Sabal palmetto	Washingtonia filifera

So, even if you don't live in the balmy south west corner of the region, there remains a good choice open to you. For adding a little flavour of the tropics to your garden, nothing quite compares to a palm.

Torbay Dazzler and other
varieties are specialities of the
Torbay Garden Centre,
Paignton, Devon

Chusan Palms at Trebah

Garden Centres
&
Gardens
to visit

PARK GARDEN CENTRE

Over Lane, Almondsbury, Avon.
Tel. (0454) 612247
Fax (0454) 617559

Known as "the gardener's garden centre", Park Garden was formerly the kitchen garden to The Tower House in Knowle Park. The Hodges family became tenants of the house and 6.5 acres in 1927 (rent £1.35 per week!) and outright owners in 1947. Keith and Sue Hodges are the current proprietors, and the tradition looks safe for at least another generation, as their two sons are training in horticulture.

The centre (member of HTA) is one for all seasons and aims for the highest standards, but amongst specialist features are a small domestic garden, a rose garden, an orchard and waterfall, affording an opportunity to gauge how the plants will look in your garden. All the staff are exceptionally well trained to offer advice and information on every aspect of gardening. Indeed, the centre covers every aspect: from aquatics to garden buildings (incl. conservatories), machinery, furniture, ornaments and bookshop; plus, of course, a very wide variety of plants - any not in stock can usually be obtained, as the centre is a Hillier Premier Plant Agent. Sue Hodges is a trained florist and houseplant specialist, so these are well represented. The fencing and paving section has a full design, construction and landscaping service, and is a stockist of Hillhout timber products and the Stonemarket paving range. So, for a rewarding day out find Park Garden just off the A38, close to junction 16 of the M5.

Summary: Demonstration gardens (incl. herbs, orchard, greenhouse); water garden; helpful, courteous staff; landscaping service; coffee shop. Open: daily 9am - 6pm in summer, 9am - 5pm in winter.

FINEBUSH GARDEN CENTRE

Hay Lane, Swindon.
Tel. (0793) 853239
Fax. (0793) 852239

Rain is the gardener's best friend, but one could do without it when strolling about a garden centre. Here it matters little: most plants are displayed under large canopies, and on table tops to make viewing easier. The range of plants, 99% of which are grown in the centre's own 20-acre nursery, is very substantial, but the specialities are pelargoniums and geraniums in spring (over 150,000 from which to choose!), poinsettas in November (over 12,000), plus fuchsias and cyclamens. But on a 5-acre site there's room for much more: a quarter acre is given over to an excellent aquatic centre, where you will find rare and exotic fish; a particularly good display of planters includes an attractive Chinese 'pavilion'; the bookshop carries over 200 titles, and there are also houseplants, garden buildings and conservatories, lawn mowers, dry goods and gifts, floristry and furniture. Coming soon is a play area, and the 48-seater restaurant is to be extended, as is the car park.

A member of the HTA, Finebush was established on this site in 1988, an amalgam of two previous centres. It lies off junction 16 of the M4, towards Wroughton on the B4005.

Summary: Pelargoniums, geraniums, poinsettas, fuchsias & cyclamens are specialities; 99% of plants homegrown; excellent aquatics; interesting planters; restaurant; play area planned. Open: 9am - 6pm Mon to Sat, 5pm Sunday.

WOODBOROUGH GARDEN CENTRE & NURSERIES

Nursery Farm, Woodborough, nr Pewsey.
Tel. (0672) 851249

The Vale of Pewsey was one of the very first parts of the country to be settled by Man, being of rich soil, mild climate and fed by the River Avon. Yet today it is one of the most sparsely populated areas of southern England, and consequently a delight to live in and to visit. The Romans grew grapes here, but it was in daffodils that founder W.T. Ware made his name, after having started out with roses in 1883. To this day the 300-acre farm grows pick-your-own daffodils, tulips, vegetables and soft fruits. The spectacular fields of shimmering colour draw many visitors in spring.

Much of what is produced on the nursery finds its way to the nearby two-acre family-run garden centre (member of HTA) and its 1750 sq ft shop. Approx. one quarter of an acre is given over to display gardens, and about the same to a canopy under which a full range of quality, carefully-labelled plants is well presented. Climbers are a speciality, notably Clematis, of which some 100 varieties have been stocked. Some of the more uncommon include armandii Apple Blossom,

texensis Etoile Rose and texensis Duchess of Albany. There are also 200 sq ft of houseplants, plus floristry materials, ornaments, Asian, dry stone and terracotta pots, books, dry goods and paving. Mrs Brewin manages the centre, aided by Madge Halsey who has worked here for over 40 years.

Summary: pick-your-own at 300-acre farm; good farm shop; climbers a speciality - wide range of clematis; nice location 3 miles west of Pewsey. Open: daily from 9am to 5pm.

LAKESIDE GARDEN CENTRE

Crockerton Shopping Centre, Crockerton, nr Warminster.
Tel. (0985) 217413

A pleasant surprise awaits visitors to this unique garden centre: an unremarkable frontage yields to a covered passage with an Aladdin's Cave of gardening goodies in a 6,000 sq ft showroom to right and left; but emerge from this and one is confronted by the lovely vista of a one-acre lake, teeming with large fish and wildfowl, and edged by fine mature trees and shrubs - well worth a visit in itself. Shrubs are, in fact, something of a speciality, and conifers are also attractively displayed in contrasting groups. There's a full across-the-range selection of outdoor plants in a half-acre site, a developing choice of indoor plants, plus greenhouses, ornaments, furniture, dried flowers and a small bookshop. Aquatics are the province of knowledgeable Steve while Phil looks after garden sundries.

Lakeside shares a 2-acre car park with the shopping centre, so one can easily combine a visit with the week's shopping. Longleat with its famous lions and beautiful Stourhead Gardens are just a short drive.

Summary: lovely lake and display gardens; shrubs a speciality; huge indoor shop; information service; deliveries within 10 mile radius. Open 9am - 5pm Mon to Sat (7:30pm Thurs & Fri), 10am - 5pm Sundays.

BARTERS PLANT CENTRE

Chapmanslade, Westbury, Wilts.
(on A3098 between Westbury & Frome)
Tel. (0373) 832694
Fax (0373) 832677

The frontage, only 30 yards wide and on a bend, is easily missed, but make sure you don't, because behind it lie 35 acres, a delight to the most critical of plantsmen. Indeed, selling nothing but plants or planting materials, Barters could be said to be a plantsman's plant centre - it is a major wholesale supplier to the West Country - but is also excellent for the novice or lazy gardener.

A particular characteristic is the enterprising manner in which plants are concept-grouped: Garden Carpets, for example - hardy perennials providing ground cover; Summer Shiners are tender or half-hardy perennials; Inside/Outside plants are selected to enhance the conservatory in winter and the patio in summer; Ferns and Bamboos for the shady corners. There's a full range of trees and shrubs (including bare roots from November), herbaceous, rock and alpine, herbs and bedding, plus some unusual varieties. All are "nursery fresh", grown on the site and in outstandingly good condition. Insects are brought in weekly as part of biological control. The widest range of stock is available in September and October.

A new feature is the Potters' Garden, displaying unusual pottery containers, backed up by expert advice, or even planting up, from Legh (on Committee of HTA) and

Diane Walker and staff, as cheerful as they are knowledgeable, and taking an obvious pride in what they do - as befits Gold Medal winners at the Ebbw Vale Garden Festival of 1992.

Summary: exclusively a plant centre; concept grouping; new Potters Garden; nursery tours by arrangement; first rate staff. Open: Mon to Sat 9am - 5pm, Sunday & Bank Hols 10am - 5pm. Closed Good Friday, Christmas & Boxing Day.

Photo: David Wiltshire

STOURHEAD HOUSE & GARDEN
Stourton, nr Warminster.
Tel. (0747) 840348

The most photographed garden in the region, if not the entire country, Stourhead is the archetypal English Arcadia. Classical Greek temples, statues and marble busts are glimpsed through canopies of exotic trees and shrubs; by the large lake is a dripping grotto with a river god, and on the opposite shore a cascade. Celestial harps would not seem out of place.

The creation of wealthy banker Henry Hoare II, (from 1741-80, as a reaction against the more formal established gardens), the 40 acres have something of interest all year: daffodils and other spring flowers, followed closely by glorious rhododendrons, and the magnificent colours of trees in autumn.

Stourhead is also blessed with its own pub, the Spread Eagle, and a National Trust shop.

Open: Daily 8am - 7pm or sunset if earlier. House open.

Photo: Terence Donovan Courtesy National Trust

WOLVERCROFT NURSERY & GARDEN CENTRE

Fordingbridge Road, Alderholt, nr Fordingbridge.
Tel. (0425) 652437
Fax. (0425) 655525

Summary: friendly, not-too-large family-run centre; own nursery; clear layout; greengroceries; tearoom and play area planned. Open: Mon to Sat 9am - 5pm (Sunday 10am - 4pm) in winter; Mon to Sat 9am - 5:30pm (Sunday 10am - 4:30pm) in summer.

Situated in open countryside, this attractive centre (member of HTA) comprises four acres, of which two acres are given over to the nursery, where many of the plants are propagated and grown. A lot is achieved in a relatively small space: quality is of a very high standard, the range and selection good; the layout is excellent - clear and well labelled, grouped according to type (eg ground cover) and in alphabetical order. Most are under high net shade and shrubs are on raised beds. The Centre has a wide range of clematis. Houseplants are also stocked, and there's a floristry selection and fresh greengroceries. Seeds and other sundries, including a small range of tools, are to be found in the shop, along with a limited selection of books, oraments and quality wooden furniture.

The Centre is owned by Henry and Kate Fookes, and Brian Buckle is the knowledgeable nursery manager. They and their staff will be pleased to offer advice - they have an information desk. They have restored farm buildings on the site, and have plans to add a cottage tearoom and play area.

Photo: Verwood Studios

STEWARTS GARDEN-LANDS

Lyndhurst Road, Somerford, nr Christchurch.
Tel. (0425) 272244
Fax (0425) 279723

One must reach for the superlatives to describe this extensive complex, one of a duo with Stewarts Country Garden Centre, Broomhill, near Wimborne. A car park for 200, plus an overflow for the same number, suggests that gardeners like what they find. The 11-acre site is attractively landscaped, the 30,000 sq ft shop is airy, tidy and colourful, and throughout great attention has been paid to detail.

There's a full range of healthy-looking plants, from herbs to forest trees, many grown in Stewart's own 50-acre nursery. Many are displayed on raised benches, and the clear labelling is enhanced by useful information boards. Staff, too, are most informative, polite and enthusiastic.

Every conceivable product and service is here; some are franchised, such as the swimming pools, aquatics, landscaping, garden machinery, greenhouses and sheds. Add to this an excellent bookshop, houseplants, furniture (3,000 sq ft), ornaments, pottery and gifts, clothing, barbecues, floristry, homemade

sweets and honey, pet accessories and you see why the large car park is a necessity. Make a day out with the family; the 2,000 sq ft restaurant is pleasant and good value, there's a play area and next door a Sainsbury's!

Summary: Weekly free lectures by experts, information desk, hanging basket planting & exchange service, very comprehensive range, large restaurant, play area. Open daily 9am (10am Sunday) to 5pm.

SAXONBURY NURSERIES

56a Saxonbury Road, Tuckton, nr Bournemouth.
(take Iford Lane exit at junction of A3060 & A35. Saxonbury Road is 7th turning on right)
Tel. (0202) 423824

Tony has set up his own impressive computer-controlled water system.

Summary: Unusual location but well worth seeking out; much for the keen gardener; herbaceous perennials a speciality; delivery service; toilets. Open: 9am - 5:30pm Mon to Sat, Sunday 9:30am - 1pm.

A pleasant surprise awaits here at this quite small centre, tucked away in an unlikely situation in a residential area - access is via alleyways between the houses. But, as the photograph shows, not one square inch of the one acre site is wasted, and the health and quality of the plants are outstanding. There's a good across-the-board variety, but the speciality is surely herbaceous perennials, which are propagated by the nursery. There are also some aquatics and houseplants. All the plants are well labelled and neatly laid out.

There is just enough room for a limited but attractive selection of ornaments and containers, plus seeds and sundries. Tony and Marilyn Raisin (HTA) are the helpful proprietors, and they or staff are always ready with advice.

BEECROFT NURSERIES

Queen Anne Drive (A341), Merley, nr Wimborne.
Tel. (0202) 693705

Being on the edge of Canford Heath, plants here tend to be acid-tolerant - heathers and alpines are especially well represented. But all the plants are of a high standard, healthy and well looked after. Hanging baskets are another speciality, and three large greenhouses are used for growing on. The site occupies 1½ acres, including a 1600 sq. ft. shop, and you will find a useful general cross section of dry goods, tools, ornaments, pots and containers, floristry and houseplants. There are also conservatories on site, but sheds have to be ordered.

The centre was started by landscaper John Soffe in 1981. He passed away in 1987, since when his wife Rita, a member of the H.T.A., has continued to maintain Beecroft as a leader in a very competitive area. She or her staff are pleased to dispense advise from an information desk.

Summary: Alpines, heathers and hanging baskets are specialities. Garden shop, conservatories, house plants. Ice creams only. Car park. Open 9am to 5pm, seven days.

JAMES TREHANE & SONS Ltd, CAMELLIA NURSERY
Stapehill Road, Hampreston, nr Wimborne.
Tel. & Fax (0202) 873490

"But we had no idea it would be so large and so interesting." That is a fairly typical remark from an amazed first-time visitor to this very special family-run nursery. Under a quarter-of-an-acre of glass and in about three acres of sheltered outdoor area grows a glorious array of magnificent Camellias, approx. 350 varieties ranging in size up to the very large "instant garden" specimens, all in containers.

The business was founded in 1959 by David Trehane (son of farmer James Trehane), aided by daughter Jennifer. It was established around a natural spring which he had found in sheltered woodland, and which has a pH of 4.8 - very acidic and ideal for Camellias. Even through the droughts the spring has continued to bubble, as do the Trehanes! Their enthusiasm and eagerness to assist both the beginner and the knowledgeable is shared by the staff, and is doubtlessly the cornerstone of their success. They are internationally acknowledged as leading experts on these most regal of shrubs, and are very influential in exhibitions, competitions, committees and indeed anything at all to do with their cultivation. David (now in his 80's) has written 'Plantsman's Guide to Camellias' and the RHS Wisley Handbook on Camellias. Jennifer has been primarily responsible for the International Camellia Society's booklet 'Camellias - a Basic Guide'.

Whether you are seeking a special plant for a special occasion, something for a small town garden or for a huge estate in Scotland, or even for export, you will not find a better choice nor more expert guidance. Small plants and orders may be sent by mail order, larger consignments by special next day delivery, but a visit in person will be a rewarding experience. You will also find other compatible plants: Azaleas, Rhododendrons, Pieris, Magnolias and the famous North American Highbush Blueberries (attractive fruit-bearing tub plants).

Summary: Expert advice, enormous choice - THE place to go for Camellias. Mail order. Car park. Open Mon - Fri 9am to 4pm, weekends from mid Feb. to end Sept 10am to 4:30pm. Closed 23rd Dec. to 4th Jan.

Camellias at James Trehane & Sons Ltd

COMPTON ACRES

Canford Cliffs, Poole.
Tel. (0202) 700778
Fax (0202) 707537

"Nowhere, perhaps, among all of Man's many endeavours, do we more surely see the face of God than in a garden." If that is so then this unique garden, one of the very finest in the land, offers a rare glimpse of His glory.

It was conceived at enormous expense by financier Thomas William Simpson just after World War I. It is, in fact, not one but 10 gardens. Simpson's design was that each should be quite separate, with its own theme - a kaleidescope of world gardens. His passion for authenticity knew no bounds: the Japanese garden, for example, was designed and built entirely by Japanese artisans, and even the stones and ornaments were shipped in from Japan. Consequently it is recognised as perhaps the only true Japanese garden in Europe.

World War II was a period of sad decline - the younger gardeners were called to military service - but since then a succession of owners have restored Compton Acres to former glory. As well as the Japanese Garden, the Italian and Rock and Water Gardens are particularly memorable, but the stunning view over Poole Harbour is one nobody ever forgets.

The 10 gardens are:-

1. The Roman Garden

2. The Herbaceous Borders

3. The Italian Garden

4. The Palm Court

5. The Woodland Walk and Sub-tropical Glen

6. The Rock and Water Gardens

7. The Viewpoint

8. The Heather Dell

9. The Garden of Memory

10. The Japanese Garden

A recent (1986) addition was the collection of superb sculptures to add to the traditional bronze and marble statuary.

Open: daily from 1st March to end of October, from 10:30am - 6:30pm (dusk if earlier). Last admission 5:45pm. Saturdays least busy. Garden Centre open throughout the year. Creperie and non-alcoholic wine bar.

Japanese Garden at Compton Acres

STAPEHILL ABBEY, CRAFT & GARDENS

276 Wimborne Road West, Wimborne.
Tel. (0202) 861686

From a run down group of buildings and a derelict piece of land (once home to an order of Cistercian nuns), has arisen one of the region's more unusual attractions, recording over 100,000 visitors in the first year.

On an 87-acre site, some of which has been transformed into formal gardens, parkland and lake, is a 12,000 sq ft museum barn housing a significant collection of agricultural implements. The award-winning gardens, which were a neglected field three years ago, continue to mature. Within the two acres of walled garden is a gardener's paradise, with formal areas, cottage garden and more. Beyond are acres of lake (teeming with wildfowl), rockery, picnic area, natural woodland and a huge play area for children. An orchid house boasts dozens of varieties, as well as other tropical plants, and in the greenhouse are more unusual plants such as pineapple, sugar canes, lemon and banana trees. The latter can also be seen outdoors alongside palms and other sub-tropical species. Over 30,000 bedding plants greet the visitor, among the more uncommon being castor oil, double impatiens and salpiglossis. There's also an important collection of special fuschias supplemented by unusual hybrids.

For casual strollers, there are laburnum and wisteria walks, woodland paths and bridges, beautifully manicured lawns and herbaceous borders. Rest awhile by the rose and lavender gardens, or under the pergolas by the fountain. There is also seating overlooking the lovely rock pools, stocked with 2,000 fish; the sound of the splashing waterfall will draw you there. Behind the rockery is an orchard with an array of spring bulbs.

Open: 10am - 5pm daily in summer; Nov. to March 10am - 4pm except Mons & Tues. Coffee shop serves lunch 12 - 2pm, snacks all day. Picnic and play area. Gift shop. Facilities for disabled. Large free car park.

STEWARTS COUNTRY GARDEN CENTRE

God's Blessing Lane, Broomhill, Holt, nr Wimborne.
Tel. (0202) 882462
Fax (0202) 842127

Widely acknowledged as opening Britain's "first" garden centre (in 1953), Stewarts (H.T.A., G.C.A.) have remained at the forefront of the trade, both here and at the other site at Somerford, near Christchurch.

There could hardly be a more idyllic setting for a garden centre, but there's much more than that to bring you to this quiet, aptly named country lane. Don't miss the animals (including Vietnamese pot-bellied pigs) and do walk the Nursery Trail, which includes Jim's Pond, a butterfly garden, native plant collection and birch collection. Between June and September on Mondays, Wednesdays and Fridays tours of the nursery are organised (no charge), an opportunity to see where and how the plants for the centre are grown.

But the highly regarded centre is the mainstay. The plants are of a high standard and beautifully presented, mostly on raised benches. There's a particularly good display of greenhouses for sale, and you will also find conservatories, sheds etc, plus well laid-out garden furniture and ornaments. The bookshop and floristry are first rate, and you could also pick up china, houseplants or homemade sweets and honey - all very suitable as gifts. Naturally, in the large shop you will find a full range of gardening goods and barbecues, but note there's no garden machinery, nor aquatics, swimming pools or landscaping. As you would expect, there is an information desk and staff are well informed and amiable. The restaurant is very agreeable and good value.

Summary: Nature Trail, animals, nursery tours. Full range of healthy plants, trees and shrubs, well labelled. Wheelchair access. Restaurant.

BLANDFORD COUNTRYWISE GARDEN CENTRE

Higher Shaftesbury Road, Blandford Forum.
Tel. (0258) 459455
Fax (0258) 480912

Summary: outstanding hardware and agricultural merchandise; developing plants business; wide range of clothing, fencing. Open: 8am-5:30pm Mon to Fri (5pm Sat), 10am-4pm Sundays in summer.

There have been interesting developments here, and doubtless many more to come, since its acquisition by M. & M. White and Mrs J. Knight in January 1992. For the previous 50 years this was a well established agricultural merchant and hardware retailer, situated on the edge of an industrial estate about one mile north of the centre of Blandford. Well frequented by local farmers, it is still a treasure trove of 3,000 sq ft of miscellaneous hardware, peats, composts, fertilisers and sprays, but nowadays you will also find a developing range of good quality bedding plants and herbaceous perennials. One may also purchase a greenhouse (displayed) or a shed (not displayed). There's a good choice of dry goods: ornaments and planters are well represented, tools, paving slabs, a wide range of both wood and wire fencing, pet accessories, a number of books, an excellent range of well-displayed clothing, furniture and dried flowers. The potential is considerable, and this is one centre worth keeping an eye on. Staff are helpful; there's a carry-out service to your car and delivery within the local area.

MOGG'S OF WELLS Ltd
Cherry Orchard, Ash Lane, Wells.
Tel. (0749) 672394
Fax (0749) 678074

Although a member of the Garden Machinery Assoc. & British Hardware Federation, Mogg's has far more to offer, and could be called a full garden centre were it not for the absence of plants. For example, you will also find greenhouses (three displayed), sheds (four displayed), garden furniture, ornaments, safety clothing, a small bookshop, fishfoods, fencing, barbecue equipment, lights, sprayers, wheelbarrows, tools and seeds!

But the core of the business remains machinery, as it has done since founded in 1905 by the grandfather of Basil Mogg, who, with wife Ann and nine well trained staff, maintains the best traditions of a family-run concern. In a showroom of 4,000 sq ft (plus ½ acre outdoor) are to be found over 400 different models from every leading manufacturer, ranging from ride-on mowers to trimmers, generators, rotovators, brushcutters, chainsaws, shredders and more, in all sizes to accommodate the grandest estate or the humblest patch. Recently introduced and of special interest are the Bolens ride-on mulching cutters and Gardena automatic watering system. Backing all this up is a 10,000 sq ft workshop and store in which is housed a

first rate repair service and many thousands of spare parts, plus expert advice.

Ann Mogg writes gardening articles for the local press, as well as a regular bulletin for the Mogg's Gardening Club (why not join when you visit), which organises day trips and other activities. There's also a monthly 'lucky numbers' discount scheme.

Open: Mon to Fri 8:30am - 5:30pm, Sat 8:30am - 5pm (spares and workshop close at 1pm). Located ½ mile north of centre of Wells. Delivery service.

81

ABBOTSBURY SUB-TROPICAL GARDENS
Abbotsbury, nr Weymouth.
Tel. (0305) 871387

"But the glory of the Garden lies in more than meets the eye" - Kipling. The author's observation is nowhere more apposite than here at Abbotsbury.

The story begins in 1765, when the first countess of Ilchester built Abbotsbury Castle on a bluff overlooking Chesil Beach. That castle is now a ruin, but the garden has continued to develop, acquiring over the years many rare and exotic plants. Of particular note is a grove of ancient Camellias which are probably from the original introduction in 1792 from Japan. There are also two specimens of the rare Piccomia excelsa and a large Podocarpus.

Many of the trees and plants have been flourishing here for well over 100 years, although native to much warmer climes. The secret lies in the location: this part of the south coast enjoys more sunshine than anywhere else on the mainland, and a moderate rainfall. This helps to ripen the wood of many plants, thereby rendering them hardier than those grown in wetter areas. Other factors are the low hills which protect the site from cold northerlies, a blanketing tree canopy and the proximity to that giant radiator, the sea. In short, here is a beneficent micro-climate.

Firs port of call will probably be the walled garden; here you will find tearooms, a sunken garden and the original Victorian Garden with its huge Chusan Palms, among the tallest in Britain.

The gardens are divided in two by a stream which forms three ponds. There are many routes around the gardens, and so much to see. Exit from the Victorian Garden and you will come across a row of cannons salvaged from the Spanish Armada. Behind them is a conservatory housing plants too tender even for Abbotsbury. Turn and walk through the new Winter Garden, then right into the Secret Walk, planted with rare Chinese plants, which leads into the Himalayan Glade. Crossing the bridge will lead you to Hydrangea Walk and Azalea Path. Heading back now a right turn up Long Walk past shrub roses (with herbaceous border to your right) takes you to the New Zealand Border and formal lily ponds.

You will have earned your cup of tea while the children romp in the play area. On the way out, don't miss the South American border, plant centre and shop. You will still not have seen everything, but there's always another day!

Open: Summer daily 10am - 5pm (last admission); Winter 10am - dusk, closed Mondays.

BARRINGTON COURT GARDEN
Nr Ilminster, Somerset.
(3 miles north on B3168)
Tel. (0460) 41938

This enchanting garden was opened to the public only quite recently, but was established in the early 1920's. Designed by Gertrude Jeckyll, it is laid out in a series of three contrasting 'rooms', each with its own colour theme: oranges and reds in the Lily Garden; soft pinks and mauves in the Iris Garden; white and silver in the White Garden.

The Buss Stalls, originally used for rearing calves, now provide the ideal planting site for fragrant roses and other climbers. On the other hand there has been no change of use in the magnificent walled kitchen garden, wherein are numerous varieties of vegetables and trained wall fruits.

The house itself is built to a typical Elizabethan E-shape in mellow Ham stone, and has been restored by the Lyle family before being returned to National Trust management in 1991.

Plants and vegetables are for sale, there's a restaurant, and excellent facilities for the disabled, including a batricar and Braille guide.

Open: April - Sept, 11 am - 5.30 pm, daily except Thursday and Friday.

Photo Rick Godley. Courtesy National Trust

CLAPTON COURT GARDENS
Clapton, nr Crewkerne.
(on B3165 3 miles south of Crewkerne)
Tel. (0460) 73220/72200

It is surprising what can be done with 10 acres: formal terraces, spacious lawns, rockery rose and water gardens in one half; woodland garden, natural streams and glades in the other. Many plants and shrubs are of special botanical interest, amongst them the biggest Ash tree in mainland Britain (over 200 years old), and a fine Metasequoia over 60' tall planted in 1950 with seed from the Arnold Arboretum in America.

Clapton is also truly a garden for all seasons: a display of bulbs dazzles in the spring, the colours of autumn are glorious. Many of the plants, shrubs and trees you see are for sale in the nursery, fuchsias and pelargoniums being specialities. There is also rare container clematis.

Homemade lunches and cream teas are normally served in the licensed restaurant during open hours. Special rates apply to coach and private parties, and parking is free. No dogs are permitted.

Open: March to October, 10:30am - 5pm Mon to Fri, Sundays 2 - 5pm, Easter Saturday 2 - 5pm (no other Saturdays). House not open.

OTTER NURSERIES Ltd

Gosford Road, Ottery St Mary, Devon.
(¹/₂ mile off A30 - turn at Pattesons Cross)
Tel. (0404) 815815
Fax (0404) 815816

One of the largest garden centres in the country, Otter Nurseries was started by Marilyn and Malcolm White, who are still running the business with the active participation of five of their children and a total staff of 160. Over the years the site has been continually developed, so that there is now a vast area under cover and every facility for a full and enjoyable day out.

The range of plants has few equals anywhere, and the stocks of shrubs, herbaceous plants, conifers and trees are quite exceptional. During the autumn a staggering 40 tonnes plus of Daffodil and Narcissi bulbs alone, in addition to many more unusual ones, are sold. Quality is also first rate: virtually all the plants are grown on the 80-acre site. The many awards won bear witness to this, including runner-up in the 'Garden Centre of the Year' competition, from over 200 alternatives. Everything you might expect to see in a garden is here, but special mention must be made of furniture: the choice is truly massive, and consequently quite difficult to make! From October until Christmas the furniture department becomes a 'Winter Wonderland' of Christmas decorations. There's also a large display of garden buildings, including conservatories, and the machinery department (with workshop) sells most makes.

The restaurant is worth a visit on its own merit. Always busy, it serves wonderful homecooked food - anything from a snack to a main meal - at very reasonable prices.

Summary: among the largest centres in the land; outstanding range of plants grown in own 80-acres; bulbs & furniture specialities; excellent restaurant; branch centre at Torquay; parking for 400 cars. Open: 9am - 5:30pm daily, except Christmas & Boxing Day.

ST. BRIDGET NURSERIES Ltd
Old Rydon Lane, Exeter.
Tel. (0392) 873672
Fax (0392) 876710

Very much a grower's nursery, this, as well as a first class general garden centre. You will find a wide selection of unusual plants, and 95% of all the trees, shrubs, roses, bedding plants, herbaceous and seasonal plants are 'home grown' in the nurseries' 100 acres and more, including rose fields which are open to the public from early July. There is also a large propagation unit in which is a micro propagation laboratory.

So there is much to interest the enthusiast, but the more casual gardener will also benefit from a day out here and at the sister branch, just two miles away at CLYST St MARY. Seasonal flowers are fresh cur for the floristry, there's a range of houseplants, and 'dry' goods in the shape of ornaments, furniture, some clothing, a bookshop, plus garden buildings etc - conservatories and patios are franchised. Children have a small play area, and you could round the day off with a pie or cream tea in the restaurant. Clyst St Mary also has an aquatic centre.

The business was established in 1925, and is now in the hands of the third generation of the same family. It is a member of the GCA, HTA, Rose Growers Association and British Association of Rose Breeders.

Summary: Own plants grown in over 100 acres; roses a speciality (fields open to public); information desk; restaurant; sister branch nearby (with aquatics). Open: Oct. to March 8am - 5pm Mon to Sat, 9am to 4:30pm Sundays & Bank Hols; March to Oct. 8am - 5:30pm, 9am - 5pm Sundays & Bank Hols.

KILLERTON GARDEN

Broadclyst, nr Exeter.
(5 miles NE of city near jnctn 28 or 29 of M5)
Tel. (0392) 881345

First laid out by Sir Thomas Acland in 1777, this memorable 22-acre garden is now owned by the National Trust. It may be divided into eight areas, each described in an informative leaflet available at the garden.

Most of the garden lies to the west of the stucco house. Nearest the house is an area laid out by William Robinson in 1905 - mixed borders (best seen in July and August) ornamented by Coade stone urns dating from 1815. There stretches out a lovely lawn, planted with numerous acid-loving trees and shrubs - magnolias, rhododendrons, maples and so on.

The Bear's Hut is a strange little edifice which was indeed once the home of a black bear, a family pet in the 19th century. Behind it is a superb rock garden, formed in a quarry excavated to build the house, and built by John Coutts, who went on to become assistant curator at Kew. Herbaceous plants such as hellebores, hostas and geraniums thrive under a canopy of camellias, maples and daphnes.

Near the marvellous glade of azaleas is The Clump, an extinct volcano, believe it or not, and also the site of an Iron Age hill fort, which you are welcome to explore.

There is much, much more to see, at any time of the year. Killerton is especially noted for its trees, including Californian Redwoods. There is also a good plant shop.

Open: 10:30am till dusk. House open daily (except Tues) from 30th March to 30th Oct. 1994, 11am - 5:30pm (last admissions 5pm).

Photo David Garner. Courtesy National Trust

MARWOOD HILL GARDENS
Barnstaple (4 miles NW by A39 & B3230).
Tel. (0271) 42528

Dr Jimmy Smart found the gardens sadly neglected when he came here in 1949, but over the years he has patiently planted and extended, so that he now has 18 beautiful acres tended by four gardeners. The stream which runs through the attractive little valley was dammed in 1969 to create an island on which is sited a fine sculpture of mother and child by Australian John Robinson.

The entrance leads to the upper garden, planted with camellias, clematis, rhododendrons, azaleas, hydrangeas, viburnum and others. A series of small waterfalls tumbles into a pool from the bank above. In a walled garden you will find plants for sale, and all around are some striking trees from various parts of the globe. Many are from the southern hemisphere, including the smallest conifer in the world from New Zealand.

Down the slope lie three small lakes, linked by streams, and between two of them is an interesting bog garden. The range of plants is too extensive to begin to list, but they thrive in appropriate habitats to provide a wonderful tapestry of colour, form and fragrance. In high summer the banks are bedecked with uncountable astilbes, a National Collection of around 135 species.

The westerly part of the garden is the most recent, developed progressively since 1977. Many fine trees are flourishing, including a belt of Japanese Larch and more of antipodean origin. On the far side of the valley is a 'Scented Arbour' and a folly - a Thollos with eight pillars housing a cherub on a seat of stone.

On top of the hill, the church provides cream teas from April to September on Sundays and Bank Holidays, and for large parties on request. There is also a large nursery, the speciality of which is camellias. A catalogue is produced but there's no mail order.

Open: Garden (not house) daily dawn to dusk. Nursery 11am - 1pm, 2pm - 5pm.

NORTH DEVON GARDEN CENTRE ASHFORD

Ashford, nr Barnstaple.
Tel. (0271) 42880
Fax (0271) 23972

On one of the most beautiful sites in the region, this is a centre worth making a long journey to visit - even if you have no particular purchase in mind. On the A361 midway between Barnstaple and Braunton, the centre lies alongside the lovely estuary, and the quite delightful tearoom (serving light lunches, cream teas etc) overlooks a lake. A two-acre show garden, started only in 1990, is already well established and continues to grow well.

With all this and a play area as well, one can enjoy a very pleasant day out with the family, but the centre, a member of the GCA and HTA, is extremely comprehensive and has everything for the serious and not-so-serious gardener. Fruit trees, of which there is an exceptionally large selection, are something of a speciality, but on this large site you will also find a full range of plants, trees and shrubs, houseplants, florist sundries, aquatics, greenhouses, conservatories and sheds, furniture, ornaments, wrought iron gates, bookshop, clothing, even bird tables. The swimming pool department covers all aspects, from site development to maintenance. The specialist aquatic centre deals in marines, tropical and cold water fish (plus associated equipment). The machinery section has a full repairs service, and there's also a landscaping service and information desk.

Established over 25 years ago, it is easy to see why this centre is one of the most popular in the area.

Summary: Stunning location; lovely tearooms; show garden; very comprehensive; fruit trees a speciality; play area; swimming pools; machine servicing; landscaping. Open: daily 9am - 5:30pm (10am - 6pm Sundays).

JACK'S PATCH GARDEN CENTRE
Newton Road, Bishopsteignton.
Tel. (0626) 776996

On the shores of the beautiful Teign estuary, the 'Patch' is in fact a very sizeable acreage of nursery and comprehensive garden centre. From humble beginnings 50 years ago, the site has developed into one of the region's best. The business remains family-run, however, by brothers Peter and Jeremy Hepworth.

For all its diversification, the garden centre also remains true to its origins as a plant specialist. The range of plants is enormous, but 85% are home-grown, and a confident 12-month guarantee is offered on all hardy plants. Staff are friendly and knowledgeable garden enthusiasts, and always keen to chat about gardening and share their knowledge.

As well as plants, there is a well-stocked gift shop, a children's playpark, a tropical and cold water fish shop and good food at 'Jack's Kitchen.'

Summary: beautiful location; plant specialist (own 6-acre nursery); friendly, knowledgeable staff; cafe; gift shop; play area; easy parking for 300.

Open: 9am - 5:30pm Mon. to Sat., 10am - 5:30pm Sun. & Bank Hols. Closes 5pm from Nov. to Feb. inclusive.

FERMOYS GARDEN CENTRE & FARM SHOP Ltd

Totnes Road, Ipplepen, Newton Abbot.
Tel. (0803) 813504
Fax (0803) 813842

Much more than just a garden centre, Fermoys is a day out for the whole family.

As the photographs show, there is a wide selection of trees, shrubs and plants (including aquatics). You will also find conservatories,

sheds, stoneware, paving and walling, outdoor ornaments and leisure furniture, bookshop, pet accessories, houseplants and a large floristry department. Staff anywhere throughout the site will be pleased to offer advice on landscaping, plant care etc.

However, there are many good reasons to visit Fermoys, even if you live in a flat without so much as a window box. An excellent farm shop offers top quality dairy products, wholefoods, fruit and vegetables - all outstandingly fresh (you can taste the difference), yet remarkably inexpensive. If that were not reason enough, there is also a superb bakery shop, a department selling fine local preserves, pasta, unusual pickles and provisions, plus a winery stocking a good choice of cider, local and other wines. Some of this wholesome and diverse provenance is bound to find its way to the 90-seater coffee shop, which serves everything from morning coffee and bacon sandwiches to light lunches, and has a range of mouthwatering homemade cakes and gateaux which would grace any sweet trolley.

Having satisfied one's alimentary needs, take time to peruse the crafts shop, where are displayed baskets, bags and many, many other handmade gifts, while the children enjoy themselves in the woodland adventure playground. Tables in this lovely natural outdoor setting provide a pleasant spot in which the whole family can savour together the above comestibles.

The large, level, wheelchair-friendly car park is a necessity: customers travel a good distance to avail themselves of all that Fermoys has to offer.

Summary: Ideal for family day out; comprehensive garden centre; excellent farm shop, bakery, winery, crafts & gifts; large coffee shop;adventure playground & woodland tea gardens. Open daily.

OTTER NURSERIES (TORBAY) Ltd

250 Babbacombe Road, Torquay.
(¹/₂ mile from Torquay Harbour, nr Palace Hotel)
Tel. (0803) 214294
Fax (0803) 291481

Nestled in a sheltered disused quarry (shared with Smith's Do-It-All), this branch of Otter Nurseries was opened in 1984. The long-established sister (or should it be mother?) centre is at Ottery St Mary, where all the plants are grown, delivered daily.

Although a smaller site, the car park accommodates 300 vehicles, and the good sized shop stocks a full range of chemicals and other gardening requisites. The range of plants is also sizeable, as are the seasonal displays of furniture, bulbs and Christmas goods. Of special note is the excellent floristry (run by Fran, wife of manager Keith Powell), affiliated to British Teleflower, which makes daily deliveries of fresh flowers and eye-catching arrangements throughout the Torbay area. Houseplants and garden ornaments are also well represented.

Summary: convenient situation and large car park; plants from own nursery; excellent floristry. Open: 9am - 5:30pm Mon to Sat, 10am - 5pm Sun. Closed Christmas and Boxing Day.

STYLES GARDEN CENTRE

Moles Lane, Marldon, nr Paignton.
Tel. (0803) 873056
Fax (0803) 872435

Summary: two centres; very attractive layout; noted for quality hardys, fruit trees, house plants, garden buildings; cafe & play area at Marldon. Open: 9am (10am Sundays) - 5pm daily.

Established over 30 years, this is one of a duo, the other being Styles at Park Hill Cross, Ipplepen (nr Newton Abbot), tel. (0803) 812495, managed by Shaun Samways. Les Harding manages Marldon, and can boast one of the most attractive layouts you are likely to see at any garden centre. The wide range of first quality plants, shrubs and trees is graded according to size, eg shrubs under two feet, over three feet and so on. There's no particular speciality, but Styles centres enjoy a fine reputation for varied, healthy hardy plants, fruit trees in season and very good houseplants. There's an outstanding selection of garden buildings, plus conservatories (at Marldon only), aquatics, machinery, furniture, ornaments, floristry, books and clothing. Marldon also has a cafe and play area.

As professional gardeners (members of GCA & HTA), Styles are able to test the products they sell and can thus make personal recommendations. Each centre has an information desk, and service is always friendly and courteous.

TORBAY GARDEN CENTRE
Brixham Road, Paignton.
Tel. (0803) 559768
Fax (0803) 665506

'The English Riviera' is famed for its palm trees, and indeed many other species of a sub tropical nature which cannot be grown in other, less fortunate parts of the country. So it is fitting that here is a garden centre where West Country palms are a principal speciality. A wide selection is available throughout the year, and several new coloured palms are unique to this centre.

Cape Marigolds (Osteospermums) are another speciality, but you will also find a good range of the more regular plants, plus aquatics, garden buildings (incl. conservatories), machinery, ornaments, some furniture, bookshop, houseplants, pets and accessories. And to help you keep fit whilst traversing this hilly region, you can even buy a mountain bike!

There's no cafeteria as such, but free coffee is laid on for all, which exemplifies the personal, quality service, giving it an edge in some ways over larger centres. A member of the HTA, the centre of course has an information desk, where one can benefit from expert and specific advice on selection, growing, after care etc, and there is a landscaping service.

Established 30 years ago, this is one of the first garden centres in the country, and remains an important port of call for those wishing to make the most of the region's unique opportunities to grow exotic plants.

Summary: Palms (some unique) and Cape Marigolds a speciality; personal service; landscaping service; free coffee. Open: Mon to Sat 9am - 5:30pm (Sunday 10am - 5:30pm). Open until 8pm Thurs & Fri in Summer.

ENDSLEIGH GARDEN CENTRE
Ivybridge.
Tel. (0752) 892254
Fax (0752) 690284

One of the region's biggest and most frequented garden centres, Endsleigh was established some 20 years ago and occupies no less than eight acres, including 40,000 sq ft under cover. Here you will find a range of specialist operators covering every conceivable requisite. Among them is one of the largest water garden suppliers in the country, swimming pools, garden buildings and conservatories, a pet shop, a patio department, garden design and landscaping, a mower specialist and even mountain bikes! Garden furniture is a forte - the choice is enormous - and there's also a full quota of garden decor and barbecue equipment. For the indoor gardener there's a floristry and excellent display of houseplants.

Special mention must be made of the Plantation Tea Shop: no plastic food with seating to match - quality is the watchword, which extends to the local produce for sale (preserves, cakes, biscuits etc).

With all this plus a children's play area, Endsleigh is obviously a great place for a day out with the family, but as a member of the HTA and Garden Centres Association it is also one for the serious gardener. The layout is first rate, and all the plants are clearly identified. As well as a landscaping service, there are four information centres dispensing advice on plant selection, nurturing, soil, location etc.

Summary: 'Comprehensive' is an understatement! Very big in aquatics and garden furniture. Landscaping. Play area. Parking for 500. Open daily 9am to 5pm (from 10am Sundays) in winter, 9am (10am Sundays) to 6pm in summer.

PLYMOUTH GARDEN CENTRE

Bowden Battery, Fort Austin Ave, Crownhill, Plymouth.
Tel. (0752) 771820
Florist (0752) 703684

Summary: Unique location; town gardens a speciality; good floristry; delivery service. Open: Winter Mon to Sat 9am - 5pm (Sunday 10:30am - 5pm); Spring & Summer Mon to Sat 9am - 5:30pm (Sunday 10:30am - 5:30pm).

Surely unique as the only garden centre in the land to be located inside a fort (one of the Palmerston Forts of the 1860's which ring Plymouth), this family-run concern may be found by following Leigham Road off the A38 over the traffic lights to the top of the hill, into the Crownhill area.

Established 30 years ago, it is personally managed by the Newton family, and is a member of the GCA and HTA. They specialise in the town garden, with particular emphasis on climbing and wall plants, container and patio plants, both perennial and seasonal. But there's also room enough in this sheltered spot for a patio centre, garden buildings (incl. conservatories), some machinery, furniture, ornaments, bookshop, houseplants, play area and car park, plus an information desk and full in-store floristry.

DUCHY OF CORNWALL NURSERIES

Penlyne Cott Road, Lostwithiel.
Tel. (0208) 872668
Fax (0579) 345672

It is not only the royal connection (Prince Charles is Duke of Cornwall) that marks this 12-acre nursery as special: as the back cover shows, it is a lovely spot for a stroll and to picnic, and it is one of the country's leading centres for rare plants - enquiries come in from far and wide. The friendly staff are always eager to share their considerable knowledge. They need to be versatile, for they sell a full range: conifers, shrubs, roses, perennials, fruit trees, aquatics and much more, and in so many varieties - not just one type of buddliea, but 20, for example. Having started in 1970 as a forestry nursery, trees are still a speciality, as are coastal plants and those suitable for milder areas. Yet for all this, prices are most competitive.

There is a move to organic methods, employing natural pest controls which include a cat on the payroll to keep down rodents!

Summary: lovely woodland walks and wildlife pond; trees & coastal plants are specialities; house plants; bookshop; friendly expert advice (member of HTA and other professional bodies); car park, toilets. Open 9am - 5pm, Mon to Sat, 10am - 5pm Sun.

Photo: Clemens Photography, Bodmin

TREWITHEN GARDENS

Grampound Road, Truro.
Tel. (0726) 883647
Fax (0726) 882301

Trewithen is Cornish for 'the House in the Spinney', appropriate enough back in 1904 when George Johnstone, who was responsible for much of what we see today, inherited the estate. His forebears had, over two centuries, planted many fine trees; indeed, it was necessary for Johnstone to thin them out in order to give other plants a chance.

World War I was responsible for the felling of 300 beeches (by government order), but it allowed Johnstone an opportunity to create the wonderful glade which still stretches southwards over 200 yards from the front of the house. Flanking both sides are rarities from all over the world, but especially Asia, collected from the wild by botanical expeditions of the 19th and early 20th centuries.

Camellias are very much a forte, including C. 'Donation' from which all the others in the world have been taken. There is also a great variety of magnolias, hosts of rhododendrons (including the marvellous yellow R. macabeanum, said to be the finest specimen in the Western

World), and many birches and maples.

There is much else besides in the 28 acres, including an admirable walled garden. Allow at least two hours for a tour, and be sure to pick up the attractive little guide book, with a map and colour photos. There is also a video presentation, plus plant centre, picnic and play area.

Open: March to September, Mon to Sat 10am - 4:30pm. House open.

ANTONY HOUSE & GARDENS

Torpoint, nr Plymouth.
(5 miles west, by A374)
Tel. (0752) 812191

In silver Petewan stone, 18th-century Antony House is one of the most striking in the West Country, and enjoys a perfect harmony with the gardens around it - thanks, in part, to the genius of Humphrey Repton. He it was who, working for the Carew family (who had owned the estate since Elizabethan times), established the lawns sweeping from the north front of the house, and cleared gaps in the trees to afford glimpses of the lovely Tamar estuary.

The garden has continued to evolve down the years. In modern times Sir John Carew introduced many exotic shrubs, rhododendrons, magnolias and over 300 varieties of camellias. He also cleared a series of grassy walks and little glades filled with spring flowers. His son, Richard, continues to develop the estate, although the house and immediate gardens were made over to the National Trust in 1961.

It is impossible to describe here all that there is to see in this marvellous 25-acre garden. Of special note are the many borders of day lilies; Antony holds part of the National Collection, and several varieties have been developed here. Against the wall of the west lawn grows a 30ft Loquat tree which produces lusciously fragrant flowers in winter. To the south is a giant cork oak, the largest in Britain. Be sure to take the 'Walks' - Yew, Lilac and Magnolia - and you can't miss the magnificent black walnut on the main lawn. To the east of the Terraces lies an oriental pond, inspired by Sir Reginald Pole Carew's visit to Japan in 1911.

Adjoining the National Trust garden is the Woodland Garden, containing over 300 camellias, a refuge for all kinds of wildlife. Here you will find lily ponds, conifer dell, bath house, saltpans and much else, not least some very fine views.

Open: April to October, Tues, Wed Thurs & Bank Hols, 1:30 - 5:30pm. Sundays also in June, July & August. House open.

CARNON DOWNS GARDEN CENTRE

Quenchwell Road, Carnon Downs, nr Truro TR3 6LN.
Tel. (0872) 863058
Fax (0872) 862162

Many would consider Carnon Downs to be Cornwall's premier Centre; certainly it is amongst the very largest and most comprehensive. A member of the GCA and HTA, it began as a flower farm in 1932, and has been run for the past 14 years or so by Anthony and Judith Lawrence. They and the staff take pride in service, getting to know and even befriending many customers, making all visitors feel welcome. Participation in fundraising events has established the Centre firmly in local affections. Likewise the special offers all year round on a whole range of goods: bedding plants, shrubbery, garden furniture, house plants and much else. Prices are always competitve, and hardy plants carry a one year guarantee (with receipt, and if reasonable care has been taken).

One must reach for the superlatives to describe Carnon Downs: a leading Koi centre; a full range of garden buildings and Cornwall's largest conservatory centre; the biggest range of Hozelock products in the area; a qualified engineer mans the machinery section; a working

pottery which exports all over the world; all the leading swimming pool suppliers are represented. Add to this aquatics, exotic birds, bookshop, floristry, landscaping, play area and licensed coffee shop, and you have several hours pleasantly and fruitfully filled.

Summary: VERY comprehensive range; friendly and knowledgable staff; keen prices; pet shop; large conservatory/buildings centre; licensed restaurant; play area; very good Christmas decor, including unusual trees. Open: 8am - 5pm Mon. to Fri., 9am - 5pm Sat., 10am - 5pm Sun. & Bank Hols.

TREBAH GARDEN

Mawnan Smith, nr Falmouth.
Tel. (0326) 250448
Fax (0326) 250781

"This is no pampered, pristine, prissy garden with rows of clipped hedges, close-mown striped lawns and daily raked paths. You are going to see a magnificent, old, wild and magical Cornish garden - the end product of 100 years of inspired and dedicated creation, followed by 40 years of mellowing and 10 years of love and restoration." So reads the introduction to the official guide, obviously written with a fierce pride. And few would challenge these assertions.

Trebah stands at the head of a 25-acre ravine, over 500 yards long and dropping 250ft to the glorious Helford estuary. The ravine is flanked by giant rhododendrons, many planted in the last century, a riot of colour in season. There are a number of paths to take you down to the beach (where one is welcome to swim or picnic); look for the Water Garden and the Zig-Zag, planted with a rare and beautiful collection of exotic plants, mainly from the Mediterranean. There are so many diversions: Camellia Walk, the Koi Pool, Mallard Pond, the Chusan Palms (said to be the tallest in England), but you will be followed everywhere by luscious fragrances, and be presented at every turn by the most wonderful aspect.

The garden and beach make for a marvellous day out with the family, and children will love Tarzan's Camp (enclosed within a giant tree canopy with ropes, climbing frames and slides), the Paraglide for over-fives, and the 'Trebah Trails' for young and old. There is also a garden shop which sells light refreshments. Dogs are permitted on leads.

After your visit you may be tempted to join the Garden Trust, formed by the Hibbert family in 1987 - details from the shop or enquire direct.

Open: Daily from 10:30am, last admission 5pm.

GLENDURGAN GARDEN

Helford River, Mawnan Smith, nr Falmouth.
(4 miles SW of Falmouth)
Tel. (0208) 74281

The glen is quite a deep ravine which empties into the beautiful, if temperamental, Helford River, and the view from the terrace of the house over the glen to the river beyond is quite unforgettable.

The Fox family have been the fortunate inhabitants since the 1820's, although the National Trust now owns the 25 acres. The garden is renowned as one for the plantsman, its trees, shrubs and flowers providing an ever-changing vista of texture and colour. It will be no surprise that there is a rich abundance of acid-loving rhododendrons, magnolias and camellias, but you will also find a diversity of wonderful trees, both evergreen and deciduous, including one of the largest tulip trees in the country. Secreted in the middle of it all is a large and complicated maze of cherry laurel, planted in 1833 by Alfred Fox, and an ancient pond stocked with trout.

The favourable micro-climate of Glendurgan - frosts are rare and winds are kept out - meant that peaches, citrus and other fruits once thrived here. Sadly, this has declined, but there are nevertheless many tender and exotic plant species for the enthusiast.

Open: March to October, Tuesday to Saturday & Bank Hols (not Good Friday), 10:30am - 5:30pm.

Photo: Andrew Besley. Courtesy National Trust

Glendurgan

OTHER GARDENS WORTH A VISIT

Cornwall
Bosvigo House, Truro
Caerhays Castle, nr Gorran (south of St. Austell)
Cotehele, St. Dominick, nr Saltash
County Demonstration Garden, Probus, nr Truro
Lanhydrock, nr Bodmin
Mount Edgcumbe, nr Plymouth
Trelissick, Feock, nr Truro
Trengwainton, Madron, nr Penzance
Trerice, nr Newquay

Devon
Arlington Court, Arlington, nr Barnstaple
Bicton Park, East Budleigh, nr Budleigh Salterton
Castle Drogo, Drewsteignton
Coleton Fishacre, Coleton, Kingswear, nr Dartmouth
Dartington Hall, Dartington, nr Totnes
Docton Mill, Spekes Valley, nr Hartland
Garden House, Buckland Monachorum, Yelverton, nr Tavistock
Knightshayes Court, Bolham, nr Tiverton
Overbecks Garden, Sharpitor, nr Salcombe
Rosemoor Garden, Gt. Torrington
Rowden Gardens, Brentor, nr Tavistock
Saltram, Plympton, nr Plymouth
Tapley Park, Instow, nr Bideford

Dorset
Athelhampton, nr Dorchester
Chiffchaffs, Chaffeymoor, Bourton, nr Gillingham
Cranborne Manor Gardens, Cranborne, nr Wimborne
Edmondsham House, Edmondsham, nr Wimborne
Mapperton House Garden, Beaminster
Parnham House, Beaminster
Tintinhull House, Tintinhull, nr Yeovil

Somerset & Avon
Claverton Manor, Claverton, nr Bath
Dunster Castle, Dunster, nr Minehead
East Lambrook Manor, East Lambrook, nr South Petherton
Forde Abbey, Chard
Greencombe, Porlock
Hadspen House, Castle Cary
Hestercombe, Cheddon Fitzpaine, nr Taunton
Lyte's Cary Manor, Charlton Mackrell, Somerton
Manor House, Walton-in-Gordano, nr Clevedon
Milton Lodge, nr Wells
Montacute House, Montacute

Wiltshire
Bowood, nr Calne
The Courts, Holt, nr Trowbridge
Heale House, Middle Woodford, nr Salisbury
Iford Manor, Iford, nr Bradford-on-Avon
Lackham College Gardens, Lacock, nr Chippenham
Roche Court Sculpture Garden, Winterslow, nr Salisbury

OTHER GARDEN CENTRES WORTH A VISIT

Cornwall
Burncoose & South Down Nurseries, Burncoose, Gwennap,
nr Redruth Chacewater, Truro
Plant Centre, Par Moor
Prices Garden Centre, St. Austell
Trevena Cross Nursery, Breage, nr Helston

Devon
Northam, nr Bideford
St. John's, Barnstaple
School Lane Nurseries, Gt. Torrington

Dorset
Cranborne, nr Wimborne
Haskins, Tricketts Cross, nr Ferndown
Three Legged Cross, nr Wimborne

Somerset & Avon
Browne's, Keward, nr Wells
Clapton Court, Crewkerne
Cobury, Congresbury, nr Bristol
Hadspen House, Castle Cary
Hillier, Bath
Hurrans, Keynsham, nr Bristol
Monkton Elm, West Monkton, nr Taunton
Parkers Garden & Aquatic Centre, Iron Acton
Scotts Nurseries, Merriott, nr Crewkerne

Wiltshire
Blounts Court, Studley, nr Calne
Bowood, Calne
Kennedy's, Stratton St. Margaret, nr Swindon
Whitehall, Lacock, nr Chippenham
Wilton House, Wilton, nr Salisbury

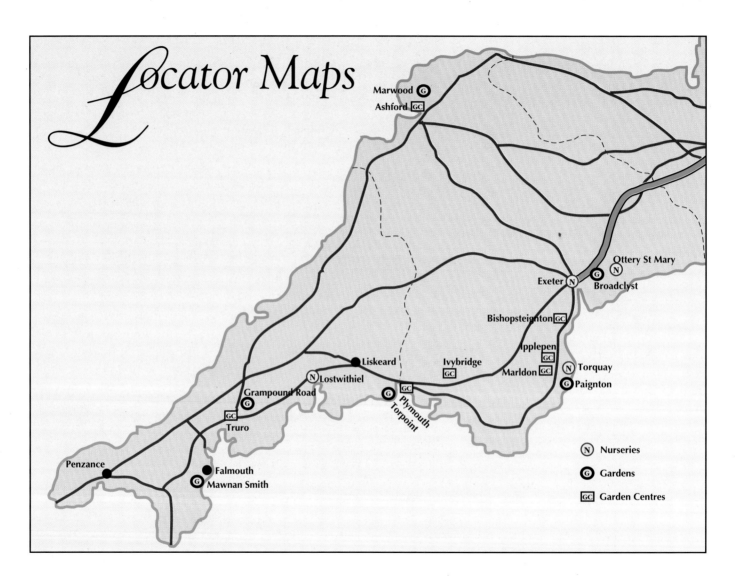

*L*ocator Maps

Marwood
Ashford
Penzance
Falmouth
Mawnan Smith
Truro
Grampound Road
Lostwithiel
Liskeard
Plymouth
Torpoint
Ivybridge
Marldon
Bishopsteignton
Ipplepen
Torquay
Paignton
Exeter
Broadclyst
Ottery St Mary

N Nurseries

G Gardens

GC Garden Centres

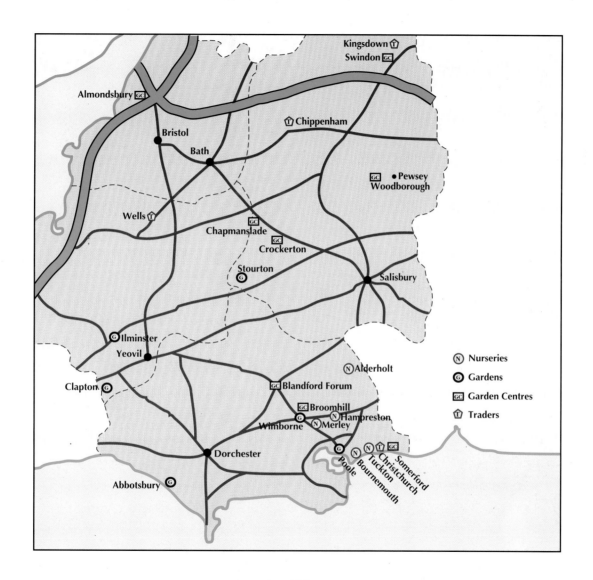

Index

Notes

Notes